SEE YOU AT THE FAR POST

Best Wishes
Terry Cochrane

Terry Cochrane

Published in 2014 by
Clive Scoular
Killyleagh
County Down

© Terry Cochrane 2014

All rights reserved. No part of this publication may be reproduced, stored in a retrieval system, or transmitted, in any form, or by any means, electronic, mechanical, photocopying, recording or otherwise, without the prior permission of the publisher and copyright holder.

ISBN 978-0-9574626-3-2

The author gratefully acknowledges the comprehensive work willingly undertaken by Clive Scoular in the writing of this book and the unstinting help given by Thomas Johnston in the preparation of the book's layout and design.

For my friends

Keith Phillips

Mick O'Neill

Kevin Healy

Tony Herlingshaw

who all died in recent years – each aged 54

I hope I'm in their team when it's time for me to go.

Photographic acknowledgements

The following are to be thanked for use of their photos:

Page 27 (bottom), Terry McArdle and John Corrigan;
Page 47 (bottom), Paul Nash;
Page 81 (bottom), The Press Association;
Page 85, the *Northern Echo*;
Page 87 (bottom), the *Northern Echo*;
Page 127, John Letley;
Page 128 (top), John Letley;
Pages 128 (bottom), Roger Triggs;
Page 129 (top), Roger Triggs.

Each of the clubs for which I played – Linfield, Coleraine, Burnley, Middlesbrough and Gillingham and the Irish Football Association – are also to be thanked for photographic contributions from their magazines and archives.

Every effort has been made to trace copyright holders. The publishers will be glad to rectify in future editions an errors or omissions brought to their attention.

Contents

Introduction 7

Imagine the scene... 9

One: Those Early Years 12

Two: Football Proper 21

Three: Irish League Football 28

Four: England and Hong Kong.. 48

Five: The International Stage.. 92

Six: Gillingham, America and Saudi Arabia 113

Seven: Professional to Amateur 131

Eight: Coaching... 136

Nine: Management at last 141

Ten: Signing Off.. 143

Introduction

My name is Terry Cochrane and I am an ex professional and international footballer. I was persuaded to write this book by my friend and former Scoutleader, Clive Scoular, who helped me write it. He is himself a successful author.

I may not have played for Manchester United, Chelsea or Arsenal but I have played for clubs who have made my life very pleasurable. I reflect upon my memories, both good and bad, at each of these clubs and the people I met there and who have remained my friends ever since. I apologise in advance to those people I have not mentioned and hope they will forgive me and realise that there is nothing personal in these omissions.

I had so many stories to tell but I could only include a few of them – some are funny and some are not.

I was a good player, but not a great one, but I was an entertainer of which there are unfortunately so few in the present day game. I gave value to each club I played for and I hope the fans thought the same. The fans at Burnley, Middlesbrough, Gillingham and all my other clubs over the years used to applaud me and it is now my turn to applaud them and thank them for their support at each of my clubs.

There is life after football.

Terry Cochrane
Middlesbrough
November 2014

Imagine the Scene...

It's Wembley stadium, London, on a Tuesday evening in May 1980. A crowd of around 35,000 rather disconsolate spectators are trudging into the terraces. These are dejected Englishmen in the main. A few smiling, or are they grinning, Northern Irishmen enter stage right. The fans take up their positions. Why are the home fans so gloomy and miserable? And why are the Northern Irishmen so perky and animated? It's the annual Home Championships involving England, Wales, Scotland and Northern Ireland – it's the end of the football season with tired and weary professional footballers looking forward to a holiday in the sun away from their exhausting and arduous training sessions. There are high expectations especially from the English fans – England will surely run away with this championship as they so often do.

But it is different this May evening – it's not England, nor Wales, not even Scotland who are making the running – it's Northern Ireland. They've already defeated Scotland. England, the mighty England, have just been trounced 4-1 by Wales. The England manager has completely changed his side making ten, yes ten, changes to his team – not exactly a sign of confidence. To the concerned English fans, their team is hardly recognisable. Northern Ireland, on the other hand, is fielding an unchanged side though the sceptics might say that they don't have such a big squad to choose from. There is tension in the air – surely this all-powerful England, even with that disastrous last result against Wales, will squash the lads in the green shirts.

The players line up in the tunnel – there is not a lot of banter – remember that the ones in the red shirts are the fearsome English and the ones of the other side are the minnows from Northern Ireland. They move out onto the pitch – there is a strange silence instead of the usual roar from the English fans. In fact the stalwart few from Northern Ireland cheer pretty loudly and can even make themselves heard above the whimpers of the home fans.

Amidst an almost deadly hush, the referee blows his whistle and the game is underway. Northern Ireland have a plan – they will resolutely defend to the death. A draw would be a good enough result – probably. So they mark and cover and tackle in their goalmouth. The English forwards do their best to sneak past the Northern Irishmen – sometimes they succeed, and make a mess of their shots, sometimes they fail and the Northern Irish, under their feisty captain, Sammy McIlroy, make a move – even as far as the halfway line. The halftime whistle goes – still no score. Some of the English fans start to leave for home or linger at the food and drink stands. They are not sure whether or not they want to return to see the rest of the game.

The second half gets underway with the Northern Irish still defending stubbornly and the English beginning to panic knowing that they only have 45 minutes to redeem themselves. The Northern Irish even begin to move forward against a very suspect English defence. Will anyone ever score? Just quarter of an hour to go – what will the morning papers say? How will the manager react? Will the fans ever return?

Then Northern Ireland make a substitution with a little over ten minutes to go – it's Terry Cochrane from Killyleagh, that talented Middlesbrough player who is taking part in his twelfth international for Northern Ireland.

Finally something happens – the English attack and the ball actually finds the net through a very fluky own goal – they are in front. A few fans cheer although it's hard to hear them. Most of the

English fans find it difficult to believe that their side has actually scored – no matter how the ball went into the net.

But within a minute Terry Cochrane races forward towards the English goal. Gerry Armstrong slides in a cross from Jimmy Nicholl right into Terry's path. He pounces on the ball and shoots it past a floundering Corrigan, the English goalie. He's scored his first international goal and it's against England. The game ends. The result is a 1-1 draw but it is surely a moral victory for the Northern Ireland team. And before the week is out Northern Ireland have triumphed in the Home Championships for the first time in 66 years. Their patience and endurance have been suitably rewarded.

The morning papers read by the dumbfounded English supporters are full of the goal by the wizard with the twinkling feet – Terry Cochrane. The Northern Irish papers are full of the story – the score might have been a 1-1 draw, but to the men and women of Northern Ireland, it's a triumphant victory for their home team.

One

Those Early days

On the 23rd of January 1953, George Terence Cochrane was born. I was the fifth child of my parents, Teresa and William John who were affectionately known as Cissie and Bill Jack. My mother was born and brought up in Bailieborough in county Cavan in the Republic of Ireland and my father, who was from Killyleagh, worked on the buses as a conductor for many years. It was through his work that he met my mother.

We lived in the lovely, picturesque village of Killyleagh on the inside shore of Strangford Lough in county Down in Northern Ireland. In the 1950s Killyleagh, though having a fairly small population, was a bustling and enterprising place. Being on the edge of the lough, there was much activity at the quay. Coal boats arrived regularly to discharge their much-needed cargo on the quayside; there were even some fishing boats still landing their catches. There was a large flax-spinning mill in the village employing many hundreds of people and close by was a shirt-making factory which was producing top class shirts for London's West End. In the nearby dormitory village of Shrigley, there was the firm of United Chrometanners which was the last remaining tannery in the whole of Ireland – there too was employed a large workforce. Added to these large employers were

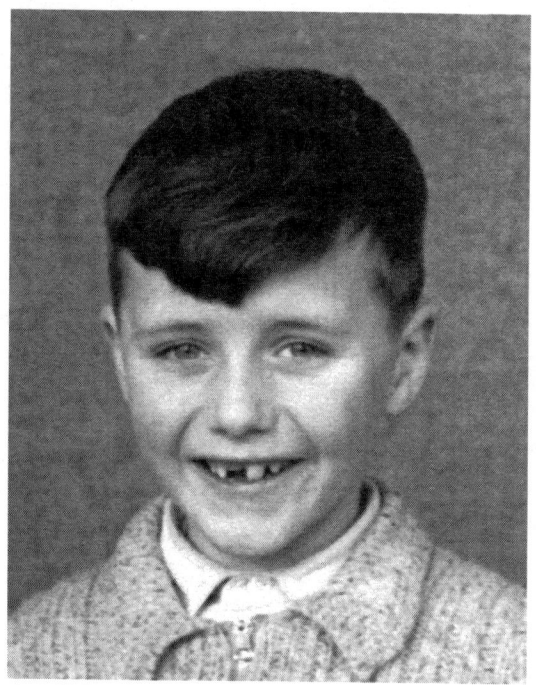

At Killyleagh Primary School when I was 7, in 1960.

lots of shops and the schools where many other locals worked. It was a very busy place as you can see.

Overlooking Killyleagh stands Killyleagh Castle, the home of the Rowan Hamilton family. It is one of the most splendid castles in the British Isles and the locals feel proud to have such a wonderful attraction in their village. The Rowan Hamiltons still live in the castle and, in my early days, we would have talked to the colonel and his wife as they shopped in the High Street. Another prominent building at the top of Church Hill, and splendidly overlooking Strangford Lough, is St John's parish church.

As a boy, like most others of my age, I suppose I didn't think of all that was going on around us. As the years went on I did of course begin to realise that the firms in the village were able to give employment to our parents and their friends. And it wasn't until many years later that I realised that some pretty great men had spent a lot of their lives in Killyleagh – people like Sir Hans Sloane who founded the British Museum and actually brought chocolate to the British Isles and also a sea captain of some importance called Sir Henry Blackwood who was there at Trafalgar with Lord Nelson. There were two other prominent men – Edward Hincks who was the rector at the parish church but who was big into reading hieroglyphics and Henry Cooke who sorted out Presbyterianism when he was in Killyleagh.

But I think the part of the village that makes me feel really proud, is the brilliant mural in Frederick Street which depicts Killyleagh's three most famous international footballers – Hugh Henry Davey, who played for Ireland from 1925 until 1928, David Healy who made 95 appearances from 2000 until 2013 and who scored 36 goals for Northern Ireland and last, but hopefully not least, Terry Cochrane, that's me, and I played for my country 26 times from 1975 until 1984. I still vividly recall the day the mural was unveiled before a big crowd of Killyleagh people and it will remain in my memory for the rest of my life. The people of Killyleagh are just the very best and I am so proud at having been honoured in this way.

My early days in Killyleagh

As I cast back my mind to the 1950s I have many vivid memories. Home was, with eight of us in the house - my three sisters, Margaret, June and Joan, and my two brothers, Noel and Hughie - a busy place. We lived at Cuan Beach, a little road which hugs the shoreline and ends up at the yacht club. It was a great location. I did get a bit involved with sailing, though not as much as I should have, but I still loved seeing the yacht races which took place regularly in the bay during the spring and summer months.

But for us boys there really only was one attraction – football. I suppose I was only five or six years old when my brothers and my friends got me involved. We played wherever there was a space to kick a ball and our favourite pitch was close to the quay end under huge piles of coal, in a kind of square that was round there. We kicked football all day and all night and I'm sure my mother had often to send someone round to chase us home. The friends I best remember joining in these sessions included Clifford and Malcolm Healy (David's father and uncle), Trevor Rea, Gary Watson, Peter Scott, Tom Healy and my brother, Hughie. We gave ourselves the names of footballers in the English League of the time and we looked forward to the days when we would all be playing professional football – it was the stuff of dreams as we passed the ball, tackled an opponent or scored a lovely goal on the hallowed turf of Old Trafford or White Hart Lane in our imagination. The reality, of course, was the dusty concrete pitch at the coal quay, but that mattered little to us – we had our dreams. Back at home, where there was yet more rivalry between Hughie and myself because he supported Manchester

United and I was a Spurs man, we even went out into the yard and kicked ball or wherever there was a space.

In 1958 I was enrolled at Killyleagh Primary School, known locally as the 'white school'. It was situated at the bottom of the hill down from the castle and was attended by, I suppose, around 100 pupils. The headmaster was Mr Maxwell Porter and one of my teachers was Mrs Olive Stevenson, who was one of our neighbours in Cuan Beach. I liked school well enough but I need hardly say that what I loved best was the opportunity to play more football. There was a good-sized playground and many of us young lads spent all our break times with the ball. There were sometimes inter class games and occasionally a game arranged by the teachers against another school. I would have enjoyed these games although I can't recall every match. All I remember is that football played an important part in my years of learning there.

When I was 11 years old, I transferred to Killyleagh High School which was very conveniently located just up behind our house – I never had to worry about being late for school for it was just two minutes away. The school never had more than about 200 pupils but the teachers attached great importance not only to learning, as you would expect, but also to improving our athletic skills. Fairly soon I got involved with the school's cross-country team. I loved it and, according to my gym teacher, Mr Eric Gourlay, I was very good at it. Over the years I won the school championship twice and was runner-up on another two occasions. In my last year at school I even won the Northern Ireland Schools Championship. I was beginning to think that this was the sport in which my future lay especially as Mr Gourlay didn't think I was much good at football. The school had a great team and many of my pals, including Russell Hagan who was a very good player, were part of it. But it was only when they were short of a man that they turned to me to play for them. In later life it seems that Eric Gourlay was surprised and dumbfounded to hear that I had become a professional footballer – I don't know what he thought when I reached the dizzy heights of playing for my country.

Scouts in Killyleagh

In the late 1960s I joined the Killyleagh Parish Scouts up at the church hall beside St John's church. Early in 1968 we welcomed a new Scoutleader, Clive Scoular. He had been brought up in Scotland but it seems had lots of Irish relatives. He was a social worker in Downpatrick and he had come to help us out when our leaders were no longer able to carry on. I suppose you could have called Clive a sort of firebrand for nothing was going to put him off. There was also the chance to play football in Scouts. In the springtime there was a district competition with the other groups in the area and we were the winners that first year. No one was happier than Clive who told me often that he could only marvel at the way I could run rings round the opposition and get up to the goal and score. We had some other great lads in our Scout team as well – Ronald and Alan Lennon, Jim Watson and William Woodside to name but a few. We made an unstoppable and unbeatable team. In May 1969, Clive entered us for the Northern Ireland Scout Football Cup which was played at Crawfordsburn, the HQ of local Scouting. It was a successful day and we emerged as winners and received the cup from the Northern Ireland international, Bryan Hamilton. It was a proud day for Killyleagh Parish Scouts and I think it would be fair to say that Clive was 'over the moon'.

Later that summer our troop headed off to Gilwell Park in London for our annual camp. It was a great place and we made lots of friends with lads from all over the country. But the story I remember best, of course, is of a football match we played with some English Scouts. I suppose they thought when they challenged us to a game that it would be a stroll – you can see their thought pattern, boys from Ireland, what do they know about football? Needless to say they were quickly disabused and shocked by our skill on that bumpy little pitch at the campsite – we easily defeated them – some would even say that we thrashed them and they went off with their tails between their legs. And something else happened on that day, 21 July 1969 – oh yes, that's it, Neil Armstrong landed on the moon.

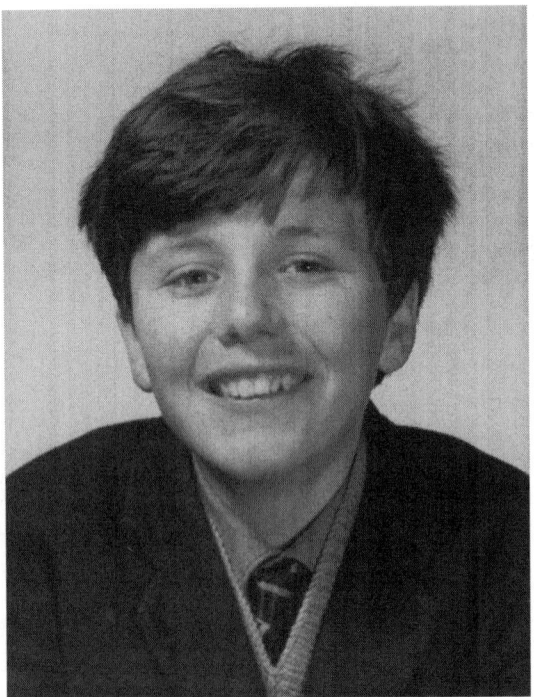

At Killyleagh High School, aged 12 in 1965.

See You at the Far Post

Playing football for the Scouts in Killyleagh, 1969.

Receiving the NI Scout Football Cup from Northern Ireland International Bryan Hamilton, May 1969.

Terry Cochrane

With Etta, Paul and Steven at home in 1982.

Two

Football Proper

The Downpatrick Youth Football League
I was determined to follow my dream. I may not have been a star player at school but I still wanted to become a member of a football team. In Downpatrick, a few miles away, there was a Youth Football League. It had started up in the late 1960s and was very popular with lots of boys. So, when I was a teenager, I went in to join one of the teams called Santos, the Brazilian club for which the maestro Pele played. All the clubs in that league had exotic sounding names. Anyway I really enjoyed my games and the training sessions with Santos at a pitch called Ibrox Park which was a pretty rough sort of place with long and uncut grass, no markings on the field and no proper goalposts. As it was quite unusual for a Killyleagh lad to play in Downpatrick, I was lucky to make friends with one of the locals on the team, Macartan Bryce. Our team manager was Charlie McStay who got us kitted out in Arsenal strips and, in the year or so I played for Santos, we won all but about two of our games. We were a slick outfit and I can remember some of those who played in the team like Charlie's twin brothers, Fred and Joe McStay, Adrian King, Neil Galbraith, Brian O'Hagan, John and Gerard Oakes, Gerard Sloan, Joe Pleasance and a lad called Jim Connelly whose nickname was 'coot'.

Terry Cochrane

Charlie was always saying that he was very glad that I was a member of his squad because I just lived for my football with a physique and talent to match. He said the main reason for this was that I had been brought up playing football whereas most of the other lads on the team had played Gaelic football in their earlier years and had only more recently taken up football. Anyway these were his words, not mine.

The weekly Downpatrick newspaper, the *Down Recorder*, regularly carried reports about the league teams and, in advance of our league's cup final with Ardglass, they predicted that I would definitely be one of the highlights of the Santos team. In the match we played exceptionally well with Macartan and myself gaining complete control of the midfield. I had a fiery temper and it seems that I started fighting on the pitch with one of the Ardglass lads called Peter Mulhall and got sent off. But I had been in devastating form in our 5-0 win, scoring the fourth and fifth goals and helping to set up the other three before being shown the red card. The report concluded that I wasn't a bad player but thought that my temperament wasn't just right. They were probably right and I knew I needed to behave myself better on the pitch. Incidentally I became a firm friend of Peter's despite my outburst with him during that game. But it was definitely during these days that I shaped all my manoeuvres and skills on the football field.

Soon afterwards Macartan and I were invited to play for the team in Castlewellan, a few miles from home. As a member of this squad, which had never before won any kind of trophy, we won the Cosmopolitan Cup. This was a summer competition organised by the Newcastle and District League with teams from Annalong, Kilkeel, Drumaness and all over mid and south Down. Big crowds watched every game, often with well over 1,000 spectators cheering on their own favourite team. In the semi final I had scored once against Banbridge and had a goal disallowed. The very next week, in the final, we beat a team called Ballyvea 8-2 and, reading the press reports of the time, I certainly had played out of my skin. 'Young Terry Cochrane completely changed the whole trend of play with three brilliant goals – this spell of sheer genius – the Ballyvea men never recovered from Cochrane's period of magic'. My friend, Charlie McStay, has recently reminded me of another amusing incident during that game. When Castlewellan were leading 4-2, Liam Magee, one of our team stalwarts, broke through the Ballyvea defence and seemed certain to score goal number five. However it seems that I appeared from nowhere, bundled Liam off the ball and rounded their keeper. Then I stopped on the line, sat on the ball with an impish grin on my face as the keeper tried to scramble back to prevent me scoring. But as he inched closer to the ball, I stood up and rolled the ball over the line. All this seems pretty typical of me at that age!

Then it happened that Macartan and I were invited to join Glentoran's youth team in Belfast although, in the end, it was Macartan who was signed and not me. There were always football scouts, in the guise of some local men, who kept an eye open for prospective professional players. One of these men, the late Bill Oakes, spotted me one evening when I was playing in an evening summer league match in Killyleagh and told me that I definitely had a future in the game – and not just in the local area but in the wider world of football. It was as if everyone already knew – I think I was the only one who didn't really believe what was happening. I had made my mark and all those goals I had scored in Downpatrick, Castlewellan and Killyleagh had led to this success. Discovering me had made Bill's day and he quickly turned promises of a professional career into practice. He arranged for me to take up an apprenticeship in July 1970 with Nottingham Forest, then managed by Matt Gillies, and even accompanied me over to England. I have a photograph from the papers showing Bill and me with the caption – 'Hero of the hour, Terry Cochrane, pictured with Mr Oakes, Nottingham Forest's chief scout, who accompanied this fine young prospect to England on Tuesday'. I even had to get my parents' permission to play for Forest's third team.

Unfortunately my trial at Nottingham did not work out because I got an injury in training. I strained a thigh muscle which was bad enough, but when the physiotherapist told me that this kind of injury could only get worse, I thought that my football career was finished before it had started. I had to return home and immediately started to attend the physiotherapy clinic at the local Downe Hospital where the dedicated work of my physiotherapist, Mrs Teggart, soon sorted me out. I was disappointed that my short apprenticeship had not worked out but I was still optimistic that I could still hopefully set off on my professional career. I was away from home for a couple of months and, although I did like the idea of going further, I thought that returning home was my best option – at this stage at any rate.

Funnily enough a year later, my friend, Macartan, also went over to Nottingham Forest and was offered an apprenticeship but turned it down.

Killyleagh Youth Club
I was not long back home when I was invited to play for my local team, Killyleagh Youth Club. Founded in 1960 the club had done remarkably well in their league and had already won a number of trophies, including, in later years, the Steel and Sons Cup. Over the years the team has been extremely successful and it still enjoys this reputation up to the present day. I enjoyed a few games with them playing alongside many of my former school friends. There were games against teams from Larne and Dundonald, for example. Reports in the papers made mention of my excellent play, but there

were quite a few of those games when we were defeated. It would be wrong to think that everywhere I played, my team won. This clearly wasn't the case but the advantage for me was that I was getting the chance to play with a number of different clubs. Although my time at the club was relatively short, probably six months or so, I had great fun with the lads there. I remember Tom Ferguson who was one of our full backs and was as hard as nails. There was also the mischievous Sammy Bennett who loved to drive our minibus to away games. Eddie Fee owned the bus but Sammy always seemed to get in behind the wheel. He drove us all crazy with his erratic and wayward driving and often enough almost got us lost including one time he got to Belfast and drove round the City Hall three or four times before someone told him where he should be going.

While I was playing for Killyleagh I had a job in the tannery in Shrigley, outside Killyleagh. Macartan was also working there, as was Bill Oakes, the football scout. At lunchtime, we would go into the yard with our work 'wellies' on, and have a game of football – and that was after having rushed home to get something to eat which my mother had prepared for both Macartan and myself. We were never going to miss any opportunity to practise our soccer skills.

I really admired the men who ran the club. They were loyal to the club and worked hard for the players. Brian Watters was the groundsman who had the pitch in terrific order week in and week out regardless of the weather. He was a lovely man and I was sorry to hear that he had died a few years ago. The managers were always dedicated and I especially remember Dee Heron who took the club to many trophies and cup wins during his time with the club. When I return to Killyleagh for a holiday I try to see as many of my old football pals as I can although, as the years pass by, more and more of them have married and left the village. But I look back on my short time with the Youth Club team with affection and remember many happy times. The club chairman, Eddie Lennon, made a presentation to me as I prepared to go for my trial with Nottingham Forest. This was typical of their kindness and affection for those, like myself, who had played well for the club. I realise that these days at Killyleagh helped set me up for my future career.

With Bill Oakes before I went for a trial to Nottingham Forest, July 1970.

See You at the Far Post

Presentation at Killyleagh Football Club before leaving for Nottingham Forest, July 1970.

Castlewellan team after winning the Cosmopolitan Cup in 1970. My friend Macartan Bryce is third from right in the back row.

Three

Irish League Football

Derry City Football Club
Early in 1969 Bill Oakes got me a trial with Derry City. To begin with I played for their reserves before eventually getting a chance in the first team under the captaincy of a very well known footballer of those days, Dougie Wood. I was delighted and realised that this was going to be quite a challenge. I was still only a teenager and I knew that if I played for this Irish League team, I would have to travel a lot between the north west and my home in Killyleagh, a distance of around 100 miles each way. But it was worth it although I do remember once missing the last bus to Killyleagh and having to walk nearly 20 miles home from Belfast. And so I became a Derry City player at the princely sum of £5 per week. At the time I had a job in Killyleagh and then one in Belfast. It was quite difficult balancing my job with my games and training sessions up in Derry but I was enjoying what I was doing and was prepared to make sacrifices for my future career.

It was actually not until 4 December 1971 that I finally got my chance to play for Derry's senior team in a league match against Glenavon. We were playing this home game at Coleraine and I scored twice in the 3-3 draw which greatly pleased me and, I suspect, the manager. I also recall a game against Linfield at Windsor Park in the spring of 1972 when we won by 2 goals to one and again I scored. A win against the mighty 'Blues' at their home ground was definitely a feather in our cap and I can tell you there were some celebrations when we returned to Derry although, when I think about it, I may have just headed straight home to Killyleagh and left the rest of the team to party. I scored five goals in that season which was a pretty good start to my football career.

I remained with Derry City until the early summer of 1972, at which time the club left the Irish League, which in effect was the Northern Irish League. The 'Troubles' were badly affecting the club and, after the trials and tribulations of having to play their home games 30 miles away in Coleraine, they decided to withdraw from the league. They played their last game at Seaview against Distillery, where they lost 2-0, under the captaincy for that final game of their long-standing goalkeeper, Eddie Mahon, with whom I had played on a number of occasions. For the next thirteen years they played junior football before joining the League of Ireland's First Division in the 1985/86 season.

For me the hand of fate again intervened when the Derry City chairman phoned me to say that Linfield Football Club were interested in signing me. I would be playing for Northern Ireland's premier football club and what's more I would be living much nearer to Belfast and would not have so far to travel.

Linfield Football Club

It certainly was a feather in my cap to be playing for Linfield, who were undoubtedly the leading club in Northern Ireland. I quickly established my place in their first team and my debut game for them was on 2 September 1972 against Crusaders at Windsor Park – a game which we lost 3-1. I made a total of 42 appearances for the club in my two full seasons with them and scored on eight occasions, including twice in a league game at the end of March 1973 against Crusaders which we won 5-1. I got on well with the lads and the management and during those years the club won a number of trophies including the Irish League in 1971, the County Antrim Shield in 1973 and the Gold Cup also in 1973. I played in these last two finals and scored in each of them. Unfortunately I didn't play in any of the club's European matches during my time at Windsor Park but I certainly looked forward to taking part in European football at some time in the not too distant future.

Whilst at Linfield I was delighted when I was offered a month's trial at Everton. The Everton manager at the time was Billy Bingham who quickly told me that I did not have the right build to be a midfielder. He told me that I was too small for them and he doubted that I would make it over in England. I never held any grudge against Mr Bingham for I knew he had a job to do. In truth I don't think it was just my skills at the game that were lacking but I rather think that, being only 18 years old, I wasn't ready to leave home and go and work in England, even if it was with a big English club. But I would meet Billy Bingham again in my professional career, as a member of his Northern Ireland international squad. I then returned to resume my career with Linfield.

The beginning of the 1970s were difficult times in Northern Ireland. I well remember training at Windsor Park one Tuesday evening when we heard gun shots at the top of the stand coming from the Andersonstown area of the city. The lights were quickly extinguished and we were taken down the tunnel to the changing rooms. Ivan McAllister was our centre half but was also a policeman and he promptly ushered us into the changing rooms. He was able to calm us down because he could clearly see that we were all scared witless – but the mood soon changed when one of the lads remarked that 'we couldn't have been playing that bad'. This funny quip took the tension out of the situation and we got on with our preparations for the next game but it was an awful shock to realise that someone was actually shooting at us in anger.

Towards the end of my time with Linfield I was beginning to wonder if the regime there was not really meant for me. I was too much of an individualist which ran contrary to what the manager, Billy Sinclair, wanted from the members of his squad. I remember once that I was dropped from the side to play our neighbours, Glentoran, in a very important final. I had been playing well, scoring and providing lots of accurate passes for my teammates to score. I could not understand his decision and I was really mad with him although, in the end, I didn't hold him any ill feelings. Like all young lads I thought I should have been selected for every team. I knew I was a temperamental type of guy and often people were taking the mickey out of me. I was normally able to deal with this but there came a time when enough was enough. This episode, along with their attitude to my forthcoming marriage, was the straw that broke the camel's back and I knew I needed to find another more welcoming set up – which soon came, thank goodness.

I got married on 13 August 1973 to a lovely girl from Killough called Etta Fitzsimons. However, since she was of a different denomination from me, the Linfield management asked me to leave the club. It actually wasn't their policy to ask a player to leave for this reason but they felt I would get too much stick if I stayed. I was pretty upset as it didn't seem any business of theirs whom I married although I did appreciate that they were a staunchly Protestant club and had been pretty honest and open with me. I would very much have liked to stay with Linfield as I was really happy there, but it was not to be.

Terry Cochrane

Coleraine Football Club

I now made my next career move. As it happened I had a visitor at my last training session at Windsor Park, Bertie Peacock, a legend of the Irish game who had played for Glasgow Celtic and was a former international for Northern Ireland. He had come to interview me to see if I would like to join Coleraine Football Club, another team in the Irish League. At that time Bertie was manager at Coleraine. I quickly accepted his offer and looked forward to yet another footballing adventure which was opening up for Etta and me. We moved to live in Coleraine where we stayed from 1973 until 1976 and it was during this time that our son, Paul, was born – on New Year's Day 1974.

The lads at the club were tremendous and the craic unbelievable. I have lots of stories from my time there and I well remember the first time I met the players after my first training session with them. A bunch of the stalwarts like Des Dickson, who had scored a hat trick against the Scottish side, Kilmarnock, in the Fairs Cup in 1970, Johnny McCurdy, Ivan Murray and Sean Dunlop, were having a drink in the bar. I interrupted them and asked if I could buy them a drink. Sean Dunlop turned to me and said 'Move away, son, there's footballers talking here'. I think this was the funniest line I had ever heard and I soon realised that the Coleraine guys had many more of these rib ticklers. I still, to this day, recall these lads with affection and fondness. It was a pleasure to be mixing with them and, of course, playing in the same team as they did. But it was a hard school.

The Coleraine team did pretty well when I was with them. In those three years I played 129 times and scored 41 goals. We won the Irish League in 1974, and the Irish Cup against Linfield in 1975 after some pretty gruelling games running up to the final in which I scored on three occasions. We also carried off the Gold Cup in 1975. Our chief rivals, apart from the Belfast duo of Linfield and Glentoran, were Ballymena United. Our fans at the Coleraine Showgrounds were always very enthusiastic, especially when any of these three teams were the opposition.

Winning that Irish Cup final against Linfield was a long drawn out affair which eventually went our way. After three attempts and 270 minutes of football, Coleraine emerged as winners. In the second match I had been suspended but was chosen to play in the third game. The fans had been enraged about my suspension and were determined that the potential match winner (i.e. me) would go ahead and win the game for Coleraine. This put a lot of pressure on me so I pleaded with them to go easy on me. They responded well and I was then able to play my part in this crucial third game. All we had to do now was win the game.

The game took place at Ballymena Showgrounds, a pitch we all knew pretty well, but a venue which displeased the Linfield management who even threatened not to play the match because they considered it an inferior pitch. We went into the match with a great record of 12 games without defeat. There had been an average of over 5,000 spectators at each of the games which, by Northern Ireland standards, was a bumper audience and there was a huge crowd again that evening. The newspapers were full of the story and the terrific play by both teams. They adjudged the man of the match as Brian Jennings and were also full of praise for my 'non stop action'. In the end we won 1-0 and the fans were jubilant. The Linfield crowd, on the other hand, took defeat badly and, as we were being presented with the cup on the field at the end of the game, a section of the Belfast fans started to throw missiles towards us. But this did not detract from our victory and there were lots of very happy looking guys in the photographs in the next day's papers. When we returned to Coleraine there were jubilant scenes of celebration from hundreds of fans who had assembled at the Showgrounds. Plenty of well-deserved praise was heaped upon Johnny McCurdy and Ivan Murray, our player managers, who had taken Coleraine to this pinnacle of footballing excellence. We were really pleased when Ivan was awarded the accolade of 'Best Player of the Year' for the second year running. And we were the last Coleraine team to win the Irish League.

I had become a favourite with the fans and was pleased at how I had played in such a great team. I was even being compared to the great George Best as 'an individualist'.

Things got better and better

Success in the cup was not just the start, but also the continuation of, some remarkable results for Coleraine Football Club. In our very next game in the league against the mighty Glentoran, I scored both goals in a 2-0 win at the Showgrounds. During the game I had sustained a bad injury to my nose and for a moment I thought it might be broken. But I was determined to play on and so I did, even with blood streaming from my nose. Thank goodness my fears were allayed when they discovered that it was only a bad bruise. And later in the game I sustained an injury to my right ankle but there was no way that I was going to leave the field.

The papers, once again, were full of superlatives about my play. 'My deadly finishing scooped both points' and 'the super-confident winger wrecked Glentoran' and again added that I was a really talented player. This may have been the case but I was quick to recognise the excellent goalkeeping skills of their man, Trevor McCullough, whose heroic acrobatics halted a rout. With our record of an unbeaten run of twenty matches in recent weeks we were ready to proudly march into Europe for our game against Eintracht Frankfurt in a couple of weeks time.

The European stage once more

We already had had a chance to play European football. In September and October 1974 we had been drawn against the Dutch side, Feyenoord, in the European Cup. We enjoyed our trip to Holland but we were thoroughly hammered in both games – defeated 7-0 away and 4-1 at home.

Now, in 1975, after we had won the Irish League title, we were drawn against Eintracht Frankfurt, but again we were soundly defeated both home and away – 5-1 in Germany – although I am pleased to say that I scored our solitary goal – and 6-2 at home when I was, once again, on the score sheet. I remember what a shock it was to the system to come out of the tunnel on to the pitch in Frankfurt to see a crowd of over 25,000 cheering German fans going wild in their immense stadium. It was quite a contrast to our much smaller home crowd of 3,000 and our modest stand at Coleraine. Our chairman, Jack Doherty, had been very proud of our performance and the way we had acted as ambassadors for both our town and for Northern Irish football. Playing in Europe, especially for the part time Coleraine team, was a great experience for all of us and, although we were not equal to the strength of the sides we played, we acquitted ourselves to the best of our ability. Playing against such well-known world soccer stars was something I never forgot. I must say that we were all pleased with the local fans and the people of Northern Ireland for the way they congratulated us on what we had achieved. You will see the photograph of the Eintracht captain, Jurgen Grabowski, which shows us swapping shirts after the home game at Coleraine.

There is a funny story about Johnny McCurdy when we were playing at Eintracht. He had had a family bereavement before we travelled to Germany and when we got there he was 'under the weather'. The club doctor was asked to keep an eye on him but, when Ivan Murray came to choose the team, which was to include

Johnny, he was nowhere to be seen. It seems the doctor had 'settled him down' a little too much and, when he eventually appeared, he was rather the worse for wear not knowing whether it was New Year or New York – needless to say, the team played without him.

Despite the disappointment of our foray into Europe, we quickly put this behind us when we took on Crusaders. We trounced them 6-0. I scored once and Ivan Murray twice. It's as well I didn't get embarrassed easily for once again the football journalists went over the top about my contribution to the win. I was 'the twinkle-toed tormentor'; 'the Crusaders defence was tangled up by my magic'; 'I danced around dangerously causing mayhem' and 'I was the shining jewel in a star-studded show'. By now Coleraine was the team of the year with so many wins under their belt and so many able, skilful and exciting players. We were definitely what the papers described as a 'polished outfit'. We knew we weren't up to European opposition but we certainly had something to aspire to. We had, after all, scored 25 goals in recent matches and only conceded three. We were the team of the moment, of that there was no doubt.

We continued our run of success in the next game, which was a Gold Cup tie, against Larne. We beat them by five goals to one and once again I scored. Despite the final score line, Larne had given us a run for our money.

Fan Mail

I never played football in the hope of getting fan mail but I really appreciated those that I did receive over the years. I still have in my possession my first fan letter which was written by a primary 4 pupil from Killowen Primary School called Robert Watten. He wrote to ask for my autograph. This is what Robert said – 'Can I have your autograph? I go to see you every week playing for Coleraine. You scored a good goal against Carrick Rangers. When Coleraine played

Glentoran and they were beaten 1-0 Coleraine should have got a lot of goals – you played great against Distillery'. I was delighted to receive Robert's letter and I, of course, obliged and sent him my signature – hopefully he still has it.

New managers at Coleraine

Bertie Peacock had resigned as manager in 1974 after thirteen years in charge, when Ivan Murray and Johnny McCurdy took over. Bertie had been very popular and was a great friend of mine. I want to mention some of the men who worked hard for the Coleraine club and especially all the work they did in the year we won the league. Jack Doherty was the chairman who was as clever as a fox and never missed a trick. I'm so thankful that he supported me financially when I hadn't a job – always remembering that Coleraine was just a part time professional club. His second in command was Hugh Wade, the salt of the earth and Raymond Pollock was another stalwart there as well. I have remained friends with these guys throughout my life.

In my final year with Coleraine I was nominated as 'Player of the Month' and my prize was a cheque for £50, which was a considerable sum in those days especially when you will be interested to know that I was earning just £9 per week as a player. I suppose players nowadays earn that amount every millisecond! This proved more than useful because at that time I had been made redundant and had no job and with my wife and young son to support. It might be difficult to appreciate that, although I was a popular player, I was still only playing football part time and only earning not much more than a pittance from the club. More and more I was hoping that sooner rather than later I would get the chance to play English football and be able to earn a decent wage. I was now 22 years old which, in terms of finding a club across the water, was getting a little bit on the old side.

I will always treasure my time spent at Coleraine and, in the meantime, I got on with the business of playing on the winning side.

A call to play for Northern Ireland

At this stage in my career I felt deep down that I was good enough to play for my country. And so did lots of other people. My name was becoming better and better known amongst the football pundits. The players and the fans at Coleraine clearly saw my enthusiasm and the skills I possessed and felt it was time for the Northern Ireland selectors to sit up and take notice of what I was achieving at Coleraine. At this time too Ivan Murray was also considered as a possible international player but he quickly set aside any of his own ambitions to promote my interests. He thought it was time for Dave Clements, the Northern Ireland manager, to call me up to his squad. However Clements remained tight-lipped as it was, of course, his right to be. He was going to be the one to make the selections and not, naturally enough, either the fans or the press. He had seen me play in lots of recent games and had clearly seen my skill and ability. According to Ivan Murray, I had never been sharper especially in the penalty area. I was ready for a call up but the call still didn't come. I was pretty philosophical about it but the fans and the management at Coleraine just could not believe that I had not been given my chance to join the Northern Ireland squad. There therefore had to be more waiting, more patience.

Soon we made a trip back to Windsor Park to play the old arch enemy, Linfield, once again. For some reason there wasn't a very big crowd which was may have had something to do with our Irish Cup win in the recent past. It was a tough game with all the players working their socks off. But early in the second half we got our chance. I broke away into the box and crossed to allow Des Dickson to score. This was the final result and the Coleraine fans and players returned home full of the joys of spring.

In the next few weeks we had two excellent wins against Larne and then Crusaders extending our undefeated run to 28 games. The game at Larne, then considered a bit of a bogey team for us, turned into a rout and we hammered them 7-0. The press even thought that we should have won by a double figure score. The Crusaders game was another easy win for us by four goals to one, and I scored a beauty in that game. Perhaps, at last, I had finally staked my claim to a place in the Northern Ireland side.

I finally got the news I had been waiting for. Dave Clements announced that I had been selected for the squad for Northern Ireland's next international match against Norway in the European Cup qualifiers in October 1975. I was delighted as were so many of my friends. Telegrams of congratulation poured into my home and to the Showgrounds. It seemed that I was the first player from a local and part time club ever to be chosen to represent Northern Ireland, which was quite an honour. I was also pleased to find myself a job in a sports outfitters, Huey and Henderson's, in Coleraine. It was nice to be able, on my first appearance in the shop, to show George Henderson and his wife, the owners, my Northern Ireland jersey. I enjoyed my experience in retail although I wasn't there for long.

That first cap

The game against Norway took place at Windsor Park in Belfast on 29 October 1975. I had, of course, already played there for Linfield but I not reckoned with the huge crowds which packed the ground that evening. The whole atmosphere was totally different to anything I had experienced before and I have to admit that I was nervous. This was a great opportunity for me. It was, after all, the achievement and realisation of my dream to play for my country.

In the game, which we won by three goals to nil, I was brought on as a substitute in the second half. It was a great thrill and I think I performed pretty well. I summed up my joy at playing for Northern Ireland in the words – 'Once you put on the green, you're a man inspired'. After the game Clements told me he had been impressed with my performance and that I was an integral part of his future plans. He indicated to me that I should maintain my high standards in the game and to continue to prove that I was every bit as good, if not better, than other prospective players who were playing in England and Scotland. So I looked forward with confidence to my next chance to play in the team but I was to be disappointed. It was another two years before I was recalled to the side. According to the soccer journalists I had played exceedingly well and they thought Clements's reasons for dropping me so quickly were flimsy and they certainly made their feelings known. But I just had to bide my time. I felt that my luck would change and eventually it did in May 1978 when Dave Clements gave me the nod once again and I was picked to play against Scotland.

See You at the Far Post

Linfield team, 1972-73 Season.

Linfield v Cliftonville, 8 September 1973.

Linfield v Ballymena, December 1972.

At Linfield, 1972-73 season.

See You at the Far Post

Coleraine – Irish League Cup winners.

Terry Cochrane

Coleraine – Winners of the Irish League Cup, 1974.

See You at the Far Post

Playing for Coleraine, 1974.

Terry Cochrane

Swapping shirts with Jurgen Grabowski of Eintracht Frankfurt, 1975.

Receiving my first International shirt, whilst at Coleraine, from Northern Ireland manager, Dave Clements, prior to the Norway match, October 1975.

Former Coleraine players who played for Northern Ireland at a function in Coleraine in April 2003.

Left to Right: Ivan Murray, Ray McCoy, Des Dickson, Hunter McClelland, Victor Hunter, Tony O'Doherty, Ray Gaston, Terry Cochrane, Bertie Peacock.

Four

England and Hong Kong

Life in the fast lane – my move to Burnley Football Club
I had really enjoyed my days at Coleraine although I was beginning to think that I would love to move to play for an English club. My player manager, Ivan Murray, believed I would soon receive such a call and it came in October 1976 from Joe Brown, the manager of the Second Division Club, Burnley. This division is equivalent to the Championship nowadays. I must admit that when I got the call, I almost got cold feet but, after talking to Etta and the club, I decided to take up the offer. A transfer fee was negotiated for £38,000 which, in those days, was a substantial sum and the highest fee paid for a part timer from Northern Ireland. I accepted and was pleased to know that from this amount Coleraine would benefit as well and help them out of some financial difficulties that they were having at the time. It would certainly help me too as I had just been paid off so this move to England saved me from the dole. The papers were full of the story – words to the effect that this 'young wizard Cochrane' would soon be thrilling the English crowds as well. All through my career I always felt a bit embarrassed by what the papers called me. I was just playing football to be best of my ability, though I suppose the journos had to write something!

When I arrived at Burnley I was immediately selected for the first team and I scored in my first two matches against Orient and Charlton. The fans were quickly taking to their Northern Irish signing and realised that 'the Clarets', as the team was known, had struck gold. It was a real thrill to be playing for this great team even though they were struggling with the prospect of relegation. We were 17th out of 22 in the league at that critical time. My arrival proved to be a lifesaver and ensured that Burnley remained in the Second Division for this season and throughout my time with them. The local newspapers and the club magazine were full of praise for the contribution I was beginning to make. They kindly acknowledged that I had saved them from a number of ignominious defeats; they delighted at my 'killer instinct'; they loved their Irish ace's 'brilliant games'. I was regularly acclaimed as the 'Claret Star', their magazine's award for the best player of the week. The fans at Turf Moor were clearly taking to me and I was warming to them and to the players at the club. Soon we had a new manager when Harry Potts took over from Joe Brown.

I still have the report of an interview with me by Peter Higgs not long after I arrived at Burnley. I was explaining the vast differences between playing in the Irish League and in the English Second Division. I described how everything at Coleraine was part time – the players, the manager, the club administrators and, above all, the training sessions we had before each week's game. The main reason for this was the fact that all the players and officials had also to hold down a job because the money we got – maybe £9 or £10 a week – would never have kept a family. I explained how much I began to appreciate the full time nature of being on the staff of an English club and how much I knew I was going to enjoy it. The other difference was, of course, the size of the crowds. At home in Coleraine the weekly gate would have been around 3,000 spectators which was a good sized crowd in Northern Ireland terms – some of the other teams in the league over there would only have had 200 or 300 at their games. I had also played in European matches back home where the numbers attending were larger. The chance now to play in front of maybe 10,000 people every week was another big learning curve for me – but I quickly embraced the experience. My parting shot in this talk with Peter was to say that I was determined and really looking forward to the tough training regime at Burnley. It was exactly what I needed – and wanted. I told him and his readers that my philosophy was to entertain the crowds and that is what I intended to do from day one.

At the start of the season I also had a couple of games with the reserves and, in a disappointing 1-1 draw with Sheffield Wednesday, I played well enough to give hope to the almost despairing fans. Soon afterwards, when I had returned to the first team, I was instrumental in bringing off a footballing miracle against Charlton Athletic. With 75 minutes of this game over, we were losing by four goals to one. But, in the last 13 minutes, we scored three times 'leaving the opposition reeling'. And I'm pleased to say that I scored 'with the crowd roaring as I angled home an incredible equaliser after perhaps the best piece of footwork of the entire afternoon'.

The 1977/78 season was pretty difficult for the club as well. We were again struggling near the relegation zone and things were beginning to look ominous. But with me doing my thing on the right wing, we won five games in a row and I was described 'as the chief architect in our recovery'. In this run of games I scored six times including 'a stunning strike' against Blackburn Rovers away from home at Ewood Park.

Then there was a League Cup game against Chester on 13 August 1977. We won this tie by two goals to nil and I scored both times. The newspaper headline described my contribution as 'spectacular' and the description of my goals went into minute detail as to how I had evaded every tackle to hammer the ball into the net. I was 'the pint sized Irishman' putting a smile back on the faces of the Burnley fans. There were always lots of action-packed photographs of me with the ball at my toe in front of the goal, ready to score.

But everything did not go totally smoothly for the Clarets. We were soundly defeated 3-0 by Sunderland in front of a crowd of 31,000 but I still received many plaudits from the reporters who described me as having been in good form. Even in defeat I was still getting the support of players and fans and, once again, I picked up the 'Claret Star'. I remember playing Stoke City in a game when we were beaten 2-1. Our chief foil that day was none other than Peter Shilton who was that first class goalkeeper for England. I was favourably mentioned in the press reports as having been most unlucky and having had my shots saved by Shilton. It seemed to me that I had made my mark at Burnley. The fans enjoyed my entertaining play and that really pleased me, but I was also very conscious of the fact that every team was made up of eleven players and each one contributed to the team's performances.

And so that season progressed. A stunning three goals to one victory over First Division Norwich City emphasised that, although we were having hiccups in our league and cup campaigns, our Burnley team was getting on top of their demons and providing ample and exciting entertainment for their fans – and keeping our manager very happy. After that game I was once again the 'Claret Star' – the man of the match with wing skills that truly delighted the crowds.

The pundits were continually complimenting me on my contributions on the field for the club. They clearly noticed how the training sessions at Turf Moor were improving my game. My positive approach to the game was greatly benefitting the club and the manager was beginning to compare me with some former England players. Peter Noble, who skippered the team and wrote some reports for the papers, was delighted with my performances and predicted that I would score more and more goals for the club and believed that I was one of the best wingers in the Second Division.

There were one or two negatives however, especially after I was cautioned for dissent over a penalty claim by the referee in the Stoke game. I was subsequently fined by the club on account of this incident. I acknowledged that I deserved what I got and tried not to let it happen again. There were other such incidents throughout my professional career and I knew I had work to do to curb my outbursts. And I'm glad to say that my on-the-pitch behaviour did improve. But, even after all this, I was still chosen as the best Burnley player on the pitch that day.

I should say at this stage that, as a pretty nifty winger, I was very often being heavily tackled by opposing defenders. This was happening all the time and, in a match against Brighton which we lost 2-1, Harry Potts was enraged at how badly I had been fouled by their Peter O'Sullivan and complained at the referee's decision not to send the Brighton man off. Even the Brighton boss, Alan Mullery, admitted that O'Sullivan's had been an awful tackle. And so, and not for the first time, I had to hobble off the field to receive attention which meant, of course, that I had to spend time in the dugout and not on the pitch.

As the season moved into 1978, things were slipping for Burnley. After our defeat by Brighton, we then had disappointing draws with Millwall and Bristol Rovers. At the Den, I was again floored by a terrible tackle, which at least resulted in our scoring from the penalty spot. Our position in the league table was once again looking decidedly precarious. The football journalists were in two minds whether to criticise us for our missed chances in recent games or to give us a bit of encouragement. I think the outcome was a bit of both. Comments about my play, however, were almost always positive and on a number of occasions I was commended for my hard work and accurate crosses which just weren't being converted into goals. They were using words like 'much improved' and even 'vastly improved' but I knew that, regardless of how well they thought I had been playing, our team needed to win more games and pick up the league points.

Thankfully our fortunes changed and we started to play very much better and our results were, for the next number of matches, absolutely fantastic. Over the weeks during March and early April towards the end of the season, we stacked up some fabulous results. From our game against Sheffield United, which we won 4-1 and where I scored twice, we actually won seven home games in a row, which probably was some sort of record for the club. We swept aside teams like bottom of the league Mansfield Town, Hull City, our third successive away win of the season, Oldham Athletic and even Spurs in various competitions including the league itself. I especially remember that Oldham game because the weather that night was atrocious and Turf Moor became nothing more than a mud bath or, as the papers described it, 'a sloshy, muddy surface best suited for armoured tank manoeuvres'. But even in these circumstances I played really well and even scored. The victory over Spurs brought an end to their unbeaten run of 19 games – another feather in our cap.

We then beat Blackburn Rovers 1-0 away from home in a torrid match where eight men were booked, not including myself I'm pleased to say, and where I scored the winner. Our last win of this excellent sequence was a 4-2 victory over Cardiff City. It was after this match that there was another push from the football journalists for me to be called up again for Northern Ireland. They suggested that I should send a memo to Danny Blanchflower reading something like 'Call me up for my country so that I can charm the Irish in the Home Internationals'. We were certainly on a high and the reporters couldn't think of great enough words to describe our run of successes and some even said that I had been the inspiration for these terrific achievements.

There was a bit of a bump towards the end of the season when both Charlton and Orient beat us but we finished off with splendid wins over Fulham and Luton Town, which meant seven home wins in a row. We had done much more than avoid relegation; we had climbed fairly high in the league. And to top it all our own Harry Potts was chosen as the best manager of the Second Division, an accolade which pleased us all and especially the fans who had, during the earlier part of the season, rather been put through the wringer.

The pundits too thought highly of my performances with such remarks as – 'very well done, Terry'. After two of those wins I was again chosen as the 'Claret Star' with such complimentary phrases as 'Burnley's most dangerous attacker' and lots of praise for my 'outstanding displays of dazzling skills'.

The 1978/79 season opened with some very positive results. In the Anglo Scottish Cup we had wins over Preston North End and Blackpool. We beat Preston by three goals to two in what was described as 'not exactly a vintage performance' but I had at least set up one of the goals. Against Blackpool we did much better and I scored the third goal in a 3-1 win. Our league programme got off to a stuttering start with three successive draws although I did score a 'cracker' in the 1-1 draw with Charlton. When the Football League Cup campaign got going, it seems that I saved the team from an ignominious defeat when I scored to salvage a draw against Fourth Division Bradford City. It was definitely the best goal I had ever scored for Burnley.

I remember playing against Glasgow Celtic in the quarter final of the 1978 Anglo Scottish Cup. This took the format of a home and an away fixture and the teams chosen to participate in this competition were the cream of the clubs in both countries. On 12 September we defeated Celtic 1-0 at home, a result which clearly did not impress the Scottish fans who caused a riot which resulted in a very ugly atmosphere for our fans and for us players. I clearly remember having a can of drink thrown at me which luckily missed. Some of the Celtic fans (or 'scum' as the Celtic manager, Billy McNeill, described them) rained bottles, iron bars and pieces of metal down on the pitch injuring a number of policemen and paramedic staff. He went out and read the riot act to the offenders and whatever he said seemed to do the trick. They calmed down after that. In the meantime many of our own fans had to take refuge on the pitch itself before the mayhem was brought under control. The referee stopped the game and brought us into the changing rooms before eventually restarting the match. This was an episode that none of us players ever wanted to happen again.

We were, as you can imagine, a bit apprehensive about our return match at Parkhead the following week but thankfully there were no further altercations. It had not been such an 'exciting' match but we won that game as well, this time by two goals to one. Unfortunately I had picked up an injury and wasn't able to play in this return match in Glasgow but I was, of course, delighted with the result for we were to go on to win the Cup against Oldham and thus added another piece of silverware to our trophy cabinet back at the club rooms at Turf Moor.

My last couple of games for Burnley turned out to be a bit of an anti-climax. Brighton beat us at home and then I was relegated to the substitutes' bench for the game against Oldham.

My career was about to take a step up and it was definitely time to leave Burnley. During my three seasons with Burnley, I had played 85 times and scored 18 goals in league, League Cup, FA Cup and other fixtures. It was always with a sense of pride that I pulled on my kit week by week to play an English League or cup match or, on a number of occasions, other competitive games against opposition from outside England. I was pleased to be known as the 'Irish Ace' – the player who had helped Burnley achieve so many fine victories against other prestigious clubs. There is a magnificent honours board at Burnley's Headquarters at Turf Moor which lists all their players who have full international caps for their home country when they were playing for Burnley and it records the four appearances I made for Northern Ireland when I was on their books.

Friends and characters I met at Burnley
Off the field I was beginning to make a number of friends especially close to my home in Brownhill Avenue. One of my great neighbours was Albert Wilkinson, the 4' 3" dwarf actor who appeared in the children's film *Wombling Free* which was based on a very popular TV programme *The Wombles of Wimbledon Common*. This proved to be a hit with almost everyone who saw the film, children and adults like myself. Over the years since he was just 14 years old Albert had acted on the stage, worked on TV programmes and had even had a role in that iconic film *Charlie and the Chocolate Factory* as one of its oompa loompas.

Albert lived a couple of doors up from us with his wife, Carol, and two daughters, Julie and Donna, and we were often in their company. In fact I clearly recall the first day we met. There was a knock at our front door and there were two lovely little girls standing on our doorstep welcoming us to the district. Soon afterwards another knock came and there was their Dad, little Albert himself, saying hello. Etta and our young son, Paul, loved having this talented and likeable man and his family as our neighbours. He even made Paul's day by presenting him with pictures of the Wombles. I think he was probably quite proud too to have a professional and international footballer living close by as well! I did like living in Burnley which to me was a homely working class town and one into which I felt I fitted, and there I stayed until I eventually moved to Middlesbrough.

Playing football for a club is just one aspect of life in that fast lane of what is professional football. What goes on before and after a match is every bit as important to one's life as the game itself. The friends I made at Burnley were a real mixture of fun and neighbourliness and I want to tell you about some of them.

Harry Potts, the manager, was a lovely man who always wore a light blue tracksuit, which didn't fit him, during our training sessions. His opening words to us every morning, come rain, snow or thunder were 'Lovely day for football'. We just smiled and got down to business.

For one of my last games playing Oldham at home, Harry put me on the substitutes' bench. I thought I deserved to be on the team and when Harry told me to get stripped and ready for the last twenty minutes of the game, I just sat there telling him that the game was terrible and that I was not going on. That was the beginning of the end of my time at Burnley. In retrospect I should not have reacted in this way – I was a professional footballer and not a prima donna. When I left the club I was really sad for they had been good to me and I did my best to make it up with Harry who had, after all, been a most conscientious manager of this premier English club. In truth I don't think Harry bore me any ill will and we parted company as good friends.

Steve Kindon was on the team with me. He was something of a joker and was always clowning around and beating up Tony Morley and myself for being cheeky. Once, on the way back on the bus from a game at Cardiff, he locked Tony in the toilet all the way back home. He was a prankster but was a great lad and everyone liked him. Nowadays I believe he is a much respected and very popular after dinner speaker at sportsmen's nights.

I have just mentioned Tony Morley who became a great friend of mine. At Burnley we vied for the wing positions but there never was any animosity because our club was always known for its ability to breed talented wingers. My funniest story about Tony happened one day in the changing room. Tony sat down beside me and said 'It's a good job the manager didn't bring me on'. I wondered why and asked the reason - 'Because I forgot to put my shorts on!' We both had a good laugh, as I really couldn't imagine a professional footballer like Tony going out on to the field of play without his shorts. He was a laid back character and a terrific teammate who later in his career was transferred to Aston Villa and won a European Cup Winners medal – I can tell you I am still mighty jealous about that.

Brian Miller was our coach whose nickname was Dusty. He was another of those guys who was always telling jokes and giving the players a 'gee up' when they needed it. But he could also get very snappy and he definitely wasn't the one to cross when we had been beaten. He'd come in to the changing room and head butt the door and then things would get very heated. But his heart was in the right place and I did like him a lot.

Dave Merrington was our youth coach and was a bit of a disciplinarian. He loved to get his lads playing with a passion and didn't like it when they were defeated. When this happened he kind of lost it and, if they were on a long bus journey home after a disappointing match, he would take to quoting the Bible at the boys. Being a Christian I expect he was trying to put them on the right path, whatever that was. The senior players like myself rather thought Dave a bit weird but this was just the type of guy he was. In his later career he moved to manage Southampton Football Club and, although I wished him well, I still couldn't believe he had landed a manager's post.

There was a great young lad called Rob Higgins who came to stay with us in Burnley. He played centre half for the reserves but was never able to make it into the first team like so many other budding football stars. When he left Burnley, he joined the police and I hope some day to be able to catch up with him for a chat about our time with the Clarets.

Middlesbrough Football Club

My soccer career now took another turn for the better. I was beginning to feel unsettled at Burnley and, as I have already mentioned, I had had a bit of a tiff with the manager over the fact that he had not played me against Oldham in one of the weeks coming up to my transfer and that he had been a bit obstructive over my request for a new contract although I did apologise to him for my action. I suppose, too, that I was getting itchy feet and I was keen to make further progress and hopefully be offered a place in a First Division club. It seems that a couple of the big clubs were showing an interest in me and one of them was Arsenal. It would have been great to sign for them, but my move ended up being to the north east and I was very happy with my upcoming prospects there.

It was towards the end of September 1978 that the manager of Middlesbrough, John Neal, approached me, as reputedly one of the top five wingers in the country, to join his club and the deal was done on that very first meeting. I was signed on the 11th of October for a record sum of £233,000, which was a staggering offer and one which both Burnley and myself jumped at. It was the third biggest sale of a player in Burnley's history, was one of the biggest transfer fees ever agreed by an English club and was a record fee for a Northern Ireland player. There is a photo in the papers showing me with a broad smile signing for the club with the caption – 'Boro boss John Neal splashed out a club record to secure the wing wizardry of tricky Terry Cochrane'. The fee really helped the dwindling finances at Burnley and also helped Coleraine for, as part of their original agreement with Burnley, they were entitled to 25% of any fee if I should move club. They received well over £50,000 which was nothing short of a massive sum for any Irish League club to be paid. Soon afterwards Coleraine built themselves a new stand at the Showgrounds and improved many of their facilities. The club was very grateful to me and there were, it seems, many of the fans who wanted this new stand to be named after me. But I am glad that they didn't do this for I never wanted such an honour.

Anyway everyone came out of the deal very well and I quickly moved to Ayresome Park and looked forward to my career in the top flight of English football. And, to add to my delight, the new Northern Ireland manager, Danny Blanchflower, after having kept me on the substitutes' bench in recent internationals, seemed to be looking more favourably at choosing me for the team. I could but wait. In the meantime I received lots of personal telegrams congratulating me on my move to the First Division. I still have them in my scrapbook and I will always greatly treasure them. And to top it all off, my second son, Steven, was born at this time.

My first game was against Norwich City which we won by two goals to nil and, although I didn't score either of them, I assisted in both. The papers were full of the story of my part in the game and it was an auspicious start for my career at Boro. It was not long before the manager and the fans began to appreciate the talents I had brought to the club. The fans quickly got behind me and they seemed to like my attitude to the game and saw me as an entertainer and crowd pleaser. The crowds were even bigger and the regular opposition of some of the greatest clubs in England like Manchester United and Chelsea spurred me on to greater and greater heights. What's more I was scoring against these mighty clubs and the fans were just loving it. I had long since banished my pre match nerves; I could not wait to play my next game. It was also in these days playing for Middlesbrough that I was regularly being chosen to play for Northern Ireland.

Week in and week out the faithful fans turned out to watch their beloved team. They were extremely passionate about their football and appreciated the expert skills of their players. A goal I scored against Chelsea is still talked about to this day and is a goal you can still see these days on YouTube. I got the ball and ran down the right wing before crossing towards the middle and sinking a left foot shot past the goalkeeper. The commentator, in his rather posh accent, described it as 'really a corker of a goal'.

Another goal I scored against Swansea is still considered to be one of the greatest goals of all time ever scored by a Middlesbrough player. It was during an FA Cup third round match at Swansea that my spectacular overhead kick put me in line for Best Goal of the Season. The BBC Match of the Day cameras were there, probably expecting us to be well beaten by the fancied Swansea side and not to capture my blistering shot. Our team was already doing well and were leading 3-0 before my scissors kick. I had my back to the goal when I considered passing it before just deciding to have a go with this unorthodox shot. My bicycle kick came off brilliantly and everyone was completely astounded at my choice of shot. Anyway it drilled past the floundering goalie and left me with a goal to forever remember. And after the game I was interviewed by David Coleman. Our assistant manager remarked that 'Terry's goal did not really surprise him for we all know what he's capable of on the football field'. This was, in retrospect, a bit of an understatement, but the sight of that ball flying over everyone's head will remain in many memory for years to come. It was my golden goal, my crowning jewel, and it still features on a club DVD to this day and talked about by the fans in the terraces. If I had a fiver for every time that someone asked me to talk about 'that' goal, I would be a very wealthy man. For the record we eventually won 5-0 leaving the highly fancied Swansea lucky to have scored nil and with lots to think about.

But as the season progressed things started to take a downward spiral. I missed a game against Bristol City after I sustained a groin injury. The club doctor gave me a tablet to relax me in order to give the muscle a chance to heal but it relaxed me too much leaving me on my back in bed for two days. Some of the fans got wind of this story and thought that I had taken too much drink the night before and couldn't play because of a hangover. This was the sort of story that did begin to give me a bit of a reputation.

However most of the fans were great with me and when I ran out on to the pitch they started to chant 'Terry, Terry Cochrane on the wing'. But at first I thought they were chanting 'Terry, Terry Cochrane on the drink'. They used to shout at me going down the wing on the chicken run end – 'Hey Terry, where are you going tonight - are you going to the Teesside dogs?', to which I replied with a quick remark, 'I'll see you there then, no problem'. These were the kind of things the fans liked and which made me try to play a bit harder.

I lost my place on the first team which frustrated me even though I realised that I was not yet one hundred per cent fit. I did not like sitting on the substitutes' bench or playing in the reserves and I'm afraid my attitude to those around me in those circumstances was not all it should have been. I was definitely feeling well below par and wondered when I would turn the corner. This meant that by the mid year of 1979 I was beginning to consider what the future held for me. I appreciated the fans' encouragement and was determined to be ready, fit and well, for the 1979/80 season. Thankfully I returned to pre season training full of the will to do well for my club. Above all the manager was delighted to see me ready for the fray for he wanted to let everyone see that his confidence in signing me was coming to fruition.

John Neal was manager for my first three years at the club. I certainly had my moments with John but I found him a bit quiet and reserved for a man in his position. Although he appreciated what I was doing for the club, I was never sure that he really liked me. I think I was too much of a doer – a mover and a shaker if you like on the football field - and he was more of a talker who seemed to lack motivation. At the beginning of my career at the club, John had the infuriating habit of only playing me at home and it was ages before I got picked for an away fixture. I never really understood his reasoning.

At Crystal Palace one day their full back, Kenny Sansom, who later went on to play for Arsenal and England, beat me at the half way line and went on to score. During the interval John rebuked me for not properly marking Sansom. I apologised to him for my mistake but went on to remind him that there were another nine men between Kenny and the goal. Once, in 1980, he fined me for what he called 'improper dress'. Why? Because I was showing my shirt rather than, I suppose, having it tucked into my shorts. However we managed to keep our relationship as friendly as we could, and moved forward until Bobby Murdoch took over the club in July 1981.

At the beginning of the New Year, 1980, Middlesbrough were on the crest of a wave. They had scored over 60 goals since the beginning of the season and in the past couple of months had only lost one game out of seven. As far as I was concerned I was once again regularly on the first team having recovered from a bit of a back injury and after serving a one match ban for some incident, the details of which I can't even remember though I must have deserved my punishment.

During January we played Portsmouth from the Fourth Division in the FA Cup. We had not done so well away from home when the score was a pretty feeble 1-1 draw although I had scored our team's goal. There had been over 30,000 spectators at that game which was a far cry from the numbers of those attending at Downpatrick and Killyleagh in my early days. Anyway the pundits knew we had had an off game and expected a hefty win at home in the replay to salvage our reputation. We surged forward and won by three goals to nil and I scored the first of our goals – I 'cracked' the ball into the net.

Around this time we took on the mighty Manchester United at Ayresome Park. The score was a 1-1 draw and the huge crowd of 30,500 (our biggest gate of the season) enjoyed a feast of wonderful football. The commentators even considered that we might get into Europe this year as well. Our own David Armstrong was playing his 330th consecutive game for Boro and was, unsurprisingly, chosen as man of the match. I seemed to have done well enough myself and I was really happy that we had taken a valuable league point off the United team.

But in truth this had been an up and down season for Boro. There had been some great results but also many where we should have done better. We even blew our chances of playing in Europe when we lost 3-1 to Stoke City in February. The manager wasn't too pleased with many of our performances. We had a great 2-2 draw with Nottingham Forest, the team I had hoped to play for earlier in my career, where our play was described as 'heroic' and where I scored one of the goals – 'crafty Cochrane' was on the ball once again. As it happens I also recall another game against Forest at the City Ground during my time with Boro. We were leading 3-0 at half time and everything was going well. They got a goal back in the second half but I think we started to back pedal letting them score two more in the last ten minutes, meaning the end result was a 3-3 draw. I rather unadvisedly told the Forest lads that they were lucky 'so and sos' and that we had let them off the hook. Then I got a tap on the shoulder from their Ian Bowyer who quietly advised me to have a look at the next day's papers and I would see that the score would still be the same – a 3-3 draw. I was speechless and slunk away with my tail between my legs. I would need to be more careful with what I said in future.

There were some not too savoury incidents during matches. I remember playing Swansea City one time when I was spat upon by their Ray Kennedy and then, in a game against Crystal Palace, their Jim Gannon did the same thing. The next bit of chew happened against Sunderland when Joe Bolton head-butted me. But, on the other hand, it would have been an exaggeration to call me a nice footballer. It was a hard game and you had to be mentally strong and give as good as you got. Present day football, with so many players coming from abroad, seems to have brought the disease into the game known as 'fall down a lot' and the British lads seem to be following their example and copying them. This, of course, confuses referees when they have to make penalty kick decisions and leads to a lot of controversy.

In May 1980 we set off to play in the Kirin Cup tournament in Japan. Jim Platt and I actually had to travel two days after the rest of the squad because of a Home International game we were to play against Wales. The whole trip was an experience none of us would ever forget and for most of us it was our first time in the land of the rising sun. Our first match was against the Japanese national side in Tokyo which we won by two goals to one. Two days later our opposition was the Argentinos Juniors team whom we defeated by four goals to nil in the city of Nagoya which is two hours away from Tokyo. We travelled there in the bullet train which was, at the time and probably still is, the fastest train in the world. This was an experience of a lifetime, I can tell you. We then went on to beat the Chinese national team by three goals to one. Our final game was against Espanol of Spain and, after drawing 0-0 after extra time, we went on to beat them on penalties. We were the winners of this prestigious competition and were mighty pleased to return home with our first piece of silverware for some time.

It was later in the season that I was picked again to play for Northern Ireland in the Home Internationals. And it was when I was on the Boro books that I won the majority of my international caps, 19 of them to be precise. In those years Boro had many fabulous wins including a 7-2 win over Chelsea, whose new manager was a very disappointed Danny Blanchflower, and a 6-0 drubbing of Norwich City. The Middlesbrough fans would well remember these triumphs but I think the Chelsea and Norwich folk would probably like to forget them.

I remained a Middlesbrough player for some years after this until 1983. I had my highs and lows but I generally was quite pleased with my time at the club. Towards the end of my time at Ayresome Park, I was called to the phone one day and told that Bobby Moore wanted to speak to me. Naturally enough I thought someone was pulling my leg but, when I did get to the phone, it really was Bobby offering me the chance to go to play in Hong Kong for a club called Eastern where he had just been appointed coach. More about this later.

As I said Bobby Murdoch, who came in 1981, was a legend amongst the supporters. He was a lovely guy and a gentleman but maybe not quite ready to be a club manager even though he was always trying to improve the team. It dawned on me that the team was beginning to slip and other big clubs were looking at our up and coming young players. Bobby was finding it hard to hold on to them and he was losing his influence on us more senior men. However I do think that we should have given him more support. An example of this was when we went to London around Christmas and New Year when we were going to play Queen's Park Rangers for the first time on their new artificial pitch. He cautioned us not to go out from our hotel, which incidentally was none other than the Waldorf, fearing that we would get up to some mischief and would not be ready for the game. However some of us, including myself, went down to the dogs at White City and made a bit of money before sneaking back to the hotel only to find the rest of the lads, with Bobby himself sitting in their midst, drinking away at the bar. So much for the manager's instructions which he was clearly flouting himself. Well I need hardly say that our training session the next morning was a disaster but, despite this, we went on to play out a very creditable 1-1 draw with QPR the next day. I think we returned home rather the worse for wear but still with a valuable league point in the bag. It just goes to show you, as the wise man said. We were all sorry when we heard that Bobby had been sacked as manager some time after this outing to London. He really hadn't done all that badly.

Malcolm Allison then took over as manager of Middlesbrough in September 1982. It would be fair to say that Malcolm and I did not get on too well. I didn't much like his attitude particularly when he expected everyone to be in awe of him, a trait which I just couldn't stomach. He was flamboyant, unorthodox and liked the limelight. He considered himself to be the saviour of the club and wanted to sort out the club and its finances. None of us players liked it when he sacked Harry, the chap who brought us our tea and whose weekly wage was all of £18, for that would only have made a tiny financial saving. He also started to bring in players who were not up to the mark in the opinion of myself and my teammates and one of them, a good enough lad in himself, Paul Sugrue, was signed because Malcolm considered him to be the best player in the Second Division. As I have said we didn't have any gripes against Paul but, as we all remarked, poor old Paul would probably wear out his shorts before his boots. Malcolm even fined me one time for what he considered 'obscene gestures' that he said I was making during a reserve team match and put me on the transfer list as well. I thought this was the most hilarious thing I was ever fined for.

Malcolm also started bringing in people to improve our coordination and physical condition. He engaged Lennie Heppell who was a British ballroom champion and I remember one Thursday in the gym at Ayresome Park we were busy trying to learn some dance steps. It was absolutely hilarious and we looked just like a lot of Bambis skating on ice. As a consequence on the following Saturday Malcolm left me, and some of the regular lads, out of the team, promising the fans an improvement in the team's performance. In the game against Blackburn Rovers we were beaten by five goals to one with me, on as a substitute, scoring our solitary goal. But we never danced again.

At that point I was just happy to leave and take the opportunity to go to Hong Kong on loan. On my return from Hong Kong I looked around for a move and found myself being signed down in Kent at Gillingham.

I had played a total of nearly one hundred games in my time at Middlesbrough but I only scored on 15 occasions. I think it would be fair to say that I was one of the most popular players the club had at that time. The fans liked me especially when I got the ball for I only ever went in one direction and that was forwards and they always cheered me on when I was on the move. But I always tried to remember that I was just one player in the team with each and every one of my teammates also doing their best.

Some other footballers at the club

Stan Cummins played for the team for a while. He was a moody lad who thought that everything and everybody was against him. He would go and look at the team sheet, which was posted up on a Friday, and if he was only listed as a substitute, he went to see the manager, John Neal. He then told John he couldn't just be a sub since the last week's Sunday papers had given him 9 out of 10 for his last performance. When the rest of the lads heard this they took the mickey out of poor little Stan for weeks afterwards.

John Coddington was our first team coach. He had recently been promoted from second team responsibilities because the side hadn't been playing so well. John had been a rugged centre half in his playing days and was a strict coach who liked training and playing us hard. One day he arrived for training after the players' annual night out at Christmas, which was something all clubs had. Alan Ramage, one of the centre halves who played in the team at the time, decided to have a bit of fun with John as we were all feeling a bit 'delicate'. John took a look at us and resolved to run the legs off us for getting into such a state. Then Alan turned to John and said 'John, I was good last night, I was drinking 'Canada Dry'. For a moment John thought, 'not bad, just lemonade'. Before he could say any more, Alan then said 'No, I started at Toronto'. Well that got the session off to a good start and you've never seen so many lads being physically sick during a training session. It was John who had the last laugh.

Stephen Bell was a young well-paid lad who was promoted by Malcolm into the first team. However everything backfired and Stephen just couldn't handle it and didn't reach the heights that many of us, including myself, thought he would. Stephen did have a gift and could have played at England level but it wasn't to be. Very sadly he died a while back and I just wanted to mention Stephen as I have a lot of fond memories of him.

Other friends and characters I met at Middlesbrough

Willie Maddren was another legend amongst the supporters and when I arrived, though he was still suffering from an injury, he took time out to show me round the area where I hoped to buy a house. Unfortunately he didn't recover from his injury, which put an end to his football career, but he remained well respected in soccer circles in Teesside. Sadly he then contracted motor neurone disease and passed away a few years back. He was one of the finest people I ever met in football.

Jimmy Meskall and his wife, Anne, became friends of ours when we arrived in Middlesbrough. We used to go to quizzes with them and went dancing in the local clubs. Jimmy and I regularly ran up in the Eston Hills with our dogs during the off-season. Sadly Anne died some time ago but I am happy to say that I am still in contact with Jimmy who, by the way, was a pretty decent footballer in his younger days.

Jimmy Walsh was godfather to Steven, our younger son, and I met him soon after arriving at Middlesbrough FC. He ran a local workingmen's club and was a friend to everyone in the area round about. We remained firm friends with Jimmy and his wife, Sheila, but sadly they too died in past years but their memory lives on with us. I have to say that Jimmy left a lasting impression upon me and I was so glad to have been numbered amongst his closest friends.

Steve Fawcett has remained one of my greatest friends over all these years. His nickname was 'Bomber' and, in the early days, was a student at Leeds University. He was a keen Boro fan and his hobby was collecting football scarves, many of them cajoled, shall we say, from visiting fans at Ayresome Park who weren't too keen to let Steve have them.

Keith Phillips was the local barber whom everybody knew. He was the kind of cheeky chappie who could have started a row in an empty house. I got to know him well and we became good friends through our mutual interest in horse racing. One day he and I were at the Pontefract races and we managed somehow or other to blag a couple of tickets from lads who were leaving the course after the first race. They weren't coming back so Keith asked them for their tickets which they gave us. We then went into the owners' and trainers' room and Keith started to chat with a group of people who were there to watch their horse which was running in the last race. In the intervening period we joined this group in conversation and a few drinks to fill in the time until the start of that last race. We decided to back their horse and, lo and behold, it won. Then I saw, to my amazement, that Keith was taking one of the ladies from the group out into the enclosure to lead the horse in. Then he managed to get me out there as well and next we found ourselves in the winner's circle. When I next looked over Keith was smartly leading the horse around accompanied by the lady and he was in every photograph being taken of the winning horse. The jockey, who was called Ray Cochrane believe it or not, dismounted and approached the lady, who was doubtless the owner, and apologised for leaving his challenge for the line a bit late even though he won of course. Before the lady had a chance to respond to her jockey, the bold Keith butted in and told Ray 'not to let it happen again'. That was my friend Keith.

And finally the boys I met at the Lambton – and Charlie Chapman
Early on I met Charlie who ran the local pub, the Lambton. He was, to me I think, the next thing to Del Boy in *Only Fools and Horses*. He

was a brash and loud Cockney and whatever came his way, he met it head on. One Sunday he sold his dinner. He came downstairs with it and the lad behind the bar said he would give him some money for it – so he did. There was another time he told this couple who had been coming in to the bar for six weeks that they could have what is called a 'stoppy back' which is letting them stay after official closing time. Little did he realise that they were CID officers and were watching Charlie having these after hours drinking sessions.

Another time he had a bit of a turn in the pub. The ambulance arrived to take Charlie to hospital. As the ambulance men were getting Charlie into the ambulance, one of the lads shouted 'Charlie, where's that tenner you were going to lend me?' It was a hard school in that pub.

I remember the first time I took Charlie to one of our Middlesbrough games. At the time I was injured so I invited Charlie into the stand. Well the relations of the players who were there nearly threw us out because, once the game had started, no one was safe from his ranting and raving. Before the end of the first half he had managed to upset all the people around us and nearly got into a row with others who were sitting a few rows away. That was the last time I took Charlie to a game.

The Lambton became the 'in' scene for my wife and myself at the weekends. We met so many good people there who befriended us not only in my playing days with Middlesbrough but also for many years later. I need to mention a few of them with fond memories, those who came to shout and cheer for me when I was playing at Middlesbrough and so this is a big 'thank you' to them. There was Brian Cassidy and his wife, Sue. Then there was 'Flapper', whose proper name I never knew, and who was another character who, without doubt, liked a drink between drinks. Then Paul and Rose Norton. Paul was a prankster who was always doing things on the guys and keeping them on their toes. He was a manager for a scaffolding company and got jobs for lots of the local lads. Then there was Kevin Healy, Mick O'Neill and Tony Herlingshaw who were some of the regulars in those days and who I got to know and I will remember them for the rest of my life.

I also knew Ted Cocker well. He took over the Lambton after Charlie left. Ted, who liked a drink of two himself, ran the pub like a home and always made everyone welcome.

Changes in the club and hopes for the future

Middlesbrough FC has changed a lot. We did gain a new chairman, Steve Gibson, who saved the club from closure in 1986. He then took the club to a new stadium at the Riverside and brought in world-class players like Juninho and Ravenelli. Under his chairmanship the club flourished with its new players, its European Cup final and its promotion from Division Two to Division One (which is now the Premiership). But all good things have now come to an end. Money has dried up because of average players coming to the Boro who are receiving wages which are scandalously high and who are not performing to the fans' satisfaction. I think that the people who were to blame for this have got away with it and have not been brought to task. They know who they are and I won't mention names. The club finished mid table in 2013 and if they don't bring in better quality players, then Boro could be in the Championship for quite a while. But, having played for the club, I hope their fortunes will turn around when they make sure they leave the dead wood behind. The fans deserve better and I know because I live among them.

Eastern Athletic Football Club, Hong Kong

As I have said I got the chance to go on loan to play for this club in Hong Kong during my last season with Middlesbrough, by which time it looked as if my contract would be coming to an end. And so I headed off on my own, as I was not allowed to bring my wife and my sons, Paul and Steven, with me. This was a real wrench for me but, with my family's support, I flew off to join my new team in this most exotic part of the world. Like most visitors flying into the old Kai Tak airport, I was a little bit apprehensive as the plane precariously weaved its way through mountains and tall skyscrapers to land, in dramatic fashion, on the runway which jutted out into the harbour. It was a thrilling introduction to my time in the Crown Colony, as it still was then.

At Gatwick airport I had met up with my playing coach, the legendary Bobby Moore, who had invited me and there he introduced me to Don Shanks who was going too. We met Bobby's girlfriend, an air hostess, who later became his wife. And then we were introduced to Don's girlfriend, Mary Stavin, who was the 1977 Miss World and who had earlier been George Best's escort in 1982. I can tell you I was speechless for to say that she was gorgeous would have been an understatement. I could only think that the boys back home would have said that I had married a welder – no disrespect, of course, to my wife.

On the plane, over a few drinks, Bobby filled us in about our new club, Eastern, how they were doing in their league and the others who were already playing for him. The squad included Graham Padden, ex West Ham United, Greg Shepherd and Roger Hansbury, both ex Norwich City, and the remainder were local Chinese players. Each team was only allowed five foreign players on the pitch at one time and so they had to depend on the Chinese lads being half decent. The football league in Hong Kong was a professional one and was totally frenetic. All the teams, and there were quite a number of them, played at the same magnificent stadium on Hong Kong Island; the top team, Seiko, had lots of Dutch players; then came Bullova with quite a few English players like Tommy Hutchinson, Barry Powell and Alan Dugdale, all ex Coventry City, and then our club, Eastern, which was the third rated team. Amongst the other clubs were the Chin Wans who had many former Brazilian stars in their squad.

The crowds at these games, and I am sure many of them watched two or three matches on the same day, were large and enthusiastic with many thousands there cheering us on. I scored in eight of the twelve games I played for Eastern and I can still recall the buzz of excitement from all the screaming fans. It was a great experience and I'm sure we all did help a lot of the local lads improve their soccer skills.

After a few months Don and I were selected to play in a Hong Kong select against Bayern Munich. We were beaten and, to add to our grief, I missed a penalty. You all know the saying that when taking a penalty, you should never change your mind but stick it where you decide. But I changed my mind and missed it. After the match I swapped shirts with Paul Breitner, Bayern's right back, who had been on Germany's winning World Cup team in 1974. I was over the moon about the shirt. When I got into the changing room, I left it down to go for a shower but when I came back it was gone. I was gutted and I'm afraid the changing room became a very loud place that night with me ranting and raving about my shirt being taken. I never did find out where it had gone.

Bobby left the club mid season because he was not receiving all the money he had been promised by the owners of the club. This left the rest of us not knowing what was going to happen now. They assured us that we would be looked after and appointed one of the Chinese coaches as chief coach. But he couldn't speak English and had to have an interpreter. Just before one of the games the interpreter told me that the Chinese coach had asked if I had any advice for the Chinese lads. 'Yes' I said 'they should sell their boots'. He seemed puzzled, at which the rest of us white lads burst out laughing for he didn't, of course, understand the joke.

The oldest club in the league was South China which was at the bottom of the league although their games were always the best attended with around 23,000 spectators. Seiko usually had 13,000, Bullova 10,000 and we at Eastern about 8,000. Games were played on a Sunday with a 4pm kick off at the main stadium on the island. Other matches were played midweek at night at Mong Kok in Kowloon on the mainland.

Before he left Bobby Moore had brought out Trevor Brooking to cover for the last three months of the contract. Trevor was the most boring person in the world in my estimation so much so that if you were cast away on a desert island with him, you would be doing your utmost to get off the island as quickly as you could for he would 'do your head in'.

There were some rather dodgy dealings amongst the Chinese lads and their managers and some of their shady actions made me turn a blind eye to what they were up to. In those days before the colony was handed back to the Chinese in 1997, football was the favourite sport amongst the local population. The clubs in the league had sister clubs and we were playing them one night. Graham Padden said we wouldn't get a result as they needed the points. We had been doing well and were third in the league but they were near the bottom. He told me that, as the owners owned both the clubs, they needed the points more than we did. I said 'Rubbish, we've been playing well and would beat them'. However just before the match the owners came in and wished us well and then had a word with the Chinese lads. Graham looked at me and said 'That's it, the owners have put the word in'. And so, to cut a long story short, we were beaten by one goal to nil and I stormed into the changing rooms very angry. Graham quietly told me to forget about it. The next thing the owners came in and gave all us 'ghoulies' (whiteys or westerners), as we were called, 1,000 Hong Kong dollars. The fix was in and I never knew about it.

Hong Kong never closed and it was a wonderful place to do all sorts of different things all day and every day. We trained either in the early morning or late in the afternoon because of the heat and humidity. Sometimes when monsoons hit and our games were postponed, we would, along with some of the other players and some jockeys whom we had got to know, go out to the racetrack. One of these jockeys was Wally Hood who came from Pontefract. He was a nice lad who gave us some tips now and again, but not many winners, I'm afraid. The lads would start at one pub and then move on to the next. By the end of the night we would have competitions with the jockeys to see who was fullest, never mind drunkest. If you had seen the state of us trying to do sit-ups, press-ups and arm wrestling, you might have thought it very funny. But it was much more serious for us since we needed to know who had come out on top – the jockey or the footballer.

In whatever other spare time I had, I was able to explore the rich culture of both the island and the mainland. I loved to travel across the harbour in the famous Star ferries when I left my hotel off the Nathan Road, the city's chief thoroughfare, and to get the chance to visit some of the lovely villages on the islands. I never had the opportunity to visit China itself which I think might have proved to be well nigh impossible anyway, but I did love to see the many wonderful sites, ancient temples and gardens which proliferate on the mainland part of the colony.

When the season finally came to an end, we finished third in the league as we had thought we would. Don, who incidentally had won a lot of money on the horses, headed back to England with me. I still had another year left on my contract with Boro but I wasn't hopeful for the future there. With Malcolm Allison, or big Mal the kiddies' pal as we called him, continuing his habit of bringing the kids into the team a bit too quickly in front of his more experienced players, I reckoned my days were numbered.

It had been a great experience being in Hong Kong, although I would have loved if my family had been able to be there with me. And it was not long before I decided to leave Middlesbrough Football Club and sign for Third Division Gillingham.

Burnley, 1976-77 season.

Terry Cochrane

First goal for Burnley v Orient, October 1976.

Burnley team, 1976-77 season.

See You at the Far Post

Burnley, second goal at home v Charlton, 1976-77 season.

In action against Middlesborough.

81

Terry Cochrane

Burnley v Millwall.

Cardiff v Burnley.

See You at the Far Post

Photoshoot for a newspaper article whilst at Burnley.

Second goal against Chester, August 1977.

Terry Cochrane

Second goal against Oldham Athletic, 1977-78 season.

Scoring against Sheffield United, 1977-78 season.

Scoring against Charlton, 1977-78 season.

Signing on for Middlesbrough, September 1978.

In action against West Brom 1978-79 season.

Terry Cochrane

In action for Middlesbrough.

See You at the Far Post

In action for Middlesbrough.

Terry Cochrane

In action for Middlesbrough.

At Middlesbrough.

Terry Cochrane

In action for Middlesbrough.

Autographed Middlesbrough card from 100 Soccer Superstars.

Five

The International Stage

My International Career

At the outset I am proud to say that I won 26 caps for Northern Ireland, thirteen of which were full caps and the other thirteen as a substitute. Eighteen of these games were away fixtures and the other eight home matches. Seven of these were played at Windsor Park in Belfast and the eighth at Hampden Park because, at that time, the 'Troubles' meant that home matches had to be played away from Northern Ireland. My career playing for my country lasted from 1975 until 1984 and involved participation in such prestigious qualifying competitions as the European Cup, the World Cup, the British Home Championship and a number of friendly matches. My chequered international career for Northern Ireland did have many ups and downs.

    I have already talked about my first game in my green shirt when I was brought on as a substitute against Norway in October 1975. I felt I had played well and so did most of the newspaper journalists – and I was still just a part timer. The Northern Ireland team that I had joined was probably the best squad out of all the eras right up to the present day with such excellent players as Pat Jennings, Sammy Nelson, Sammy McIlroy, Martin O'Neill, David McCreery,

Chris and Jimmy Nicholl, Norman Whiteside, Gerry Armstrong, Billy Hamilton, Chris McGrath and the late Noel Brotherston. This was a quality team which I think is lacking in today's squad.

But it was a further two and a half years before I got my recall. I had wondered if I would ever play for my country again but I'm pleased to say that my patience eventually bore fruit and I was recalled to the squad for the British Home Championships in 1978. This was a competition which had been played amongst the four home nations for one hundred years. It was always played at the end of the football season, usually in the months of May or June. Because of the 'Troubles' in Northern Ireland during the early 1970s, some of the other countries had refused to come to play in Belfast and this was the case in May 1978. This meant that we had to play all three games away from home in Glasgow, London and Wrexham. We lost to England and Wales and managed a 1-1 draw against Scotland where Martin O'Neill scored our solitary goal. I was on the substitutes' bench for all three games although I did play in each game for a short while. I did not score but I played well enough. This now meant that I had been chosen four times to play for Northern Ireland but had not yet played for the entire 90 minutes.

I hoped my fortunes would change when I was chosen to join the squad to play the Republic of Ireland on 20 September 1978. According to the papers my call up was a deserved reward for some scintillating football in recent weeks but, once more, I only had a few minutes' play again as a substitute. I must say that I was very frustrated as were many others who were pressing Danny Blanchflower to give me a full game. There were many who considered that Danny was past it as a manager and I think I would have agreed with their sentiments. I remember a silly incident during a game against England at Windsor Park when Gerry Armstrong and I had a bit of a 'set to'. Gerry kicked me in the backside so I just turned round and hit him. It was a clash simply borne out of frustration at the way the game had been going. We quickly apologised to one another and got on with the game for it was the sort of thing that happened from time to time on the football pitch. But at half time Danny summoned us and told us he wasn't pleased at what had happened and to behave ourselves. Then he told me to go and have a bath and so I didn't play the rest of the game. This epitomised our negative attitude to Danny for Gerry and I, and everyone else I suppose, knew perfectly well how to make up after a tiff. It wasn't appropriate for professional footballers to be acting this way but we didn't need anyone, let alone Danny Blanchflower, to be telling us off. There was another problem when Danny appointed Tommy Cavanagh as team coach. He didn't like anyone who didn't play for Manchester United because he was the coach there too – he was a right pain in the backside. When I was playing he would be saying to Danny to bring me off as had been the case, I'm sure, during the altercation between Gerry Armstrong and myself in the England game. The press even suggested that there was some religious implication in the incident which was absolute nonsense. As players we didn't care for that sort of thing and just got on with playing the game.

Looking back at this time I really did wonder why I wasn't being chosen for a full game for I had been on the squad for a long time by then. I admit that I am not the calmest of people but I somehow managed to keep my annoyance under my hat. Surely my time would come.

A Full Cap at last

My patience eventually bore fruit. Just a month after the Republic of Ireland game I was selected to play against Denmark in a European Championship match at Windsor Park – and I played as a full cap for the first time. I was delighted and determined to play out of my skin which, according to the papers, I certainly did. Before a crowd of 25,000 I gave a superb performance and ran rings round the Danish defence. We were playing well but still we managed to go a goal down. However I came to the rescue with a well set up cross to allow Derek Spence to equalise and a few minutes later we scored again through Trevor Anderson to record a 2-1 victory. As we left the field all I could hear were chants of 'we want Terry' echoing all around the ground. The papers were full of the story with lots of action photographs featuring me during the game and they were overjoyed not only about the win itself but also with my thrilling play. I was the new hero for the cheering fans who vociferously reminded the manager that I should never be side-lined again. But the reality was that it was the manager who made the decisions and not the fans. Just before the end of the game, however, I had to leave the field of play after sustaining a slight injury but I was more than content with my performance and was soon fit again.

Between November 1978 and March 1980 I was awarded five more full caps. I played against Bulgaria twice when we won both games 2-0, once in Belfast and the other in Sofia in the European Cup campaign in 1978 and 1979. It was on this occasion, when we were playing against Bulgaria, that I had a little go at the Bulgarian fullback who went down as if poleaxed. My number was up and I was substituted. Chris McGrath then came on and played in my position. Then Chris got the ball on the wing when this same fullback tackled him and down he went again. He had been elbowed in the face and lost a tooth. Down in the dugout, I spoke up, rather sarcastically, and said 'Good substitution, that could have been me'. Tommy Cavanagh, as ever, was not amused.

There were two games against England, the first of which was in February when we lost by four goals to nil. And so we had something to prove when we took them on again in May. I was awarded a full cap for this game and all the players were told to do all they could to prise open the English defence and win the game in front of our very partisan home crowd at Windsor Park. But they were to be disappointed when we lost 2-0. The message after the game from the manager was not to lose faith for we still had a decent chance of qualifying for the European Cup competition and he thought we were still doing reasonably well. Then there was a very disappointing game against Israel in March 1980 in the World Cup qualifiers, which we drew 0-0 away from home. I still had not scored for Northern Ireland although I seemed to be doing pretty well in the team. In some of these games I was substituted towards the end of the game but there was nothing unusual about that. I just kept plugging away hoping to keep my place in the team.

The British Home Championship of May 1980
As ever we were due to play against the three other home countries in this competition set for the end of May. It was a special year for the Irish League as it was their centenary year. The first game was against Scotland but I was not on the team. We won by one goal to nil which was a great start to our campaign. On the 20th we travelled over to London to take on the old enemy at the magnificent Wembley Stadium. Once again I was not chosen to start the game but just after halftime, when there still was no score, I was brought on. England had just come from a 4-1 defeat by Wales, which had truly stunned them but we were still the clear underdogs and we knew they had something to prove. Within a minute England scored through an own goal and so things weren't looking too good. It was then from a cross by Jimmy Nicholl that I scored my first goal for my country at the twelfth attempt and not just against any country, but against England. I was ecstatic. My teammates, the manager and the select number of Northern Ireland fans stood up and wildly

cheered in the midst of a crowd of over 30,000 very stunned and shamefaced Englishmen. Not many Northern Ireland players have scored against England – Terry Neill, George Best and years after me, my fellow Killyleagh pal, David Healy. I was immensely proud and, in all honesty, considered this the pinnacle of my entire footballing career – to that point at least. In a later interview I even declared that 'If you'd have killed me then, I'd have died happy!' We do say some silly things but I think, at least for a moment or two, that I really meant what I had said.

The papers, I need hardly say, were full of the story which described the draw as a tactical victory. The fans were 'tingling with pride as if coming out of a dream' and declared that Northern Ireland had soaked up the English pressure with me pouncing on the ball and squeezing it past the floundering English keeper. These days you can find almost anything on YouTube and if you search for that goal, you'll find it. To be honest I still look at it from time to time and cannot believe that it was little old me who put that ball into the English net.

On the phone immediately after the game, Etta was able to tell me that, when she was at her bingo session in the town, the MC interrupted the session to announce that I had scored. The crowd erupted in bursts of applause and cheering despite the goal having been scored against England. They were clearly proud of their local boy made good even if he had scored for his own little Northern Ireland against their mighty England.

There were some rather more negative remarks in the press but they really were just sour grapes. It was said by some detractors, mostly English I suspect, that the Home Championships were only an unwelcome intrusion into England's preparations for the European finals but I'm proud to say that the unanimous response to this moan was 'what rubbish – Northern Ireland taught the English a lesson'. Never was a truer word spoken.

The campaign went from strength to strength and, with our 1-0 win over Wales in Cardiff, we came top of the league with five points out of a possible six. Northern Ireland had won the Home Championships for the first time in 66 years. It had been a hit and run victory and had been nothing short of a miraculous week for Northern Ireland football. And just to prove it was the entire population who were congratulating us, the Lord Mayor and the City Council gave us a civic reception at the City Hall in recognition of what they called our magic and marvellous success and achievement. We were each then presented with a special gold medallion on behalf of the Irish Football Association. A large front page photograph in the evening newspapers showed us celebrating under the banner 'The Champagne Boys' – praise indeed.

International football on the other side of the world

One thing about playing international football means travelling to places where we would never dream of visiting. There were lots of great cities in Europe where I had played and I'm glad to say that I saw a bit more in those places than just the football stadium.

In June 1980 the Northern Ireland team was invited to go on tour to Australia. We were to play in Sydney, Melbourne, Adelaide and Perth. Our team which, as you can imagine was on a bit of a high after winning the Home Championship, was without some of its key players and those of us who travelled arrived in Sydney very weary after nearly two days in the air. Few of us had ever experienced such a long plane trip. However we overcame our jet lag and took to the field at the famous Sydney cricket ground with Billy's 'positive' thoughts ringing in our ears. We were in great form and won by two goals to one. I came on as a substitute replacing Noel Brotherston and acquitted myself well. In fact Billy considered that it was one of the team's greatest ever performances under his managership which was quite an accolade.

We moved on to Melbourne and, in front of a 10,000 crowd, we were held to a 1-1 draw by the Socceroos, the quaint and homely name given to the Australian football team. Again I came on as a sub and it was my pass which Gerry Armstrong turned into the Australian net. Billy wasn't so pleased at how we had played this time and went on to say that I still had the annoying habit of dwelling on the ball too long. Obviously I had still a lot to learn about international football.

Three days later we were in Adelaide and this time I got a full cap – maybe Billy wanted to see if I had heeded his advice about passing the ball rather than hanging on to it. I think I must have passed the test for the manager instructed the lads that I was to take the key role during the game. We won by two goals to one and we were all delighted that one of our goals was scored by the young Linfield star, Colin McCurdy, in his first international. Thus far we had won twice and drawn once on our antipodean tour and we felt pretty good about our performance to date. It has to be said that the Australians themselves played well in this series of matches. If we had thought that playing Australia would be a stroll in the park, we quickly realised that they were a smart outfit, thus I suppose, proving that Northern Ireland was also a footballing force with which to be reckoned.

We moved on to our fourth and final match of the tour. We arrived at Perth cricket ground just a day after there had been a freak whirlwind which caused a great deal of damage in the city and the surrounding area. In the game, which we won by the confortable margin of four goals to nil, I scored the second and third goals which pleased me immensely with the local papers describing my contribution as skilful and industrious. But I was then to receive a bit of a shock for, as Murphy's or Sod's law would have it, this game was not deemed to have been a full international for some obscure reason meaning that my goals would not count as international goals as it had been adjudged as a 'friendly' fixture. I had played my heart out in the other three games, which were full internationals, but did not find the net. I had enjoyed my experiences in Australia but I did feel a little 'hard done by' when my goals at Perth could not be added to my international tally.

The 1982 World Cup campaign
The World Cup was due to take place in Spain in the summer of 1982. The number of teams to qualify had been increased from 16 to 24 thus making Northern Ireland's chances of qualifying much greater. And the team was playing very well now under their recalled manager, Billy Bingham, who had himself been a member of the squad in the 1958 World Cup finals and who had previously managed the team between 1967 and 1971. The first matches were held early in 1980, over two years before the finals. Northern Ireland had a fairly tough draw with Sweden, Portugal, Scotland and, rather surprisingly since they weren't even members of UEFA, Israel. I was almost certain to be picked for the squad as I had been playing so well. I have already mentioned the discouraging draw in Tel Aviv with Israel in early 1980 but by the end of the year, we were due to play both Sweden and Portugal. I played in the majority of the games although I was just used as a substitute in these first two games. We comfortably won the match against Sweden at Windsor Park by three goals to nil. This was a most convincing performance as we sent the Swedes reeling, an apt description according to the papers. Although I was just brought on as a substitute I felt that I had helped the side to this memorable victory. Billy Bingham was congratulated for the way he had been able to bind his new young team together

and at the end of the game he declared that it had been Northern Ireland's best display since he had taken over as manager. In fact it had been a most successful run with nine games without defeat. It had been a long time since we had scored such success but we knew we could not be complacent.

We now confidently hoped for something maybe even better in Lisbon against Portugal in November. However, although we played to the best of our ability, we lost this game 1-0. I had come on in the second half and tried all I could to salvage the situation but sadly to no avail. Some of the commentators called my play a bit laboured which didn't please me at all. Losing the game therefore left our chances of qualification a bit on a knife-edge although our fans and supporters encouraged us not to get too desperate and pessimistic. In the following March we drew 1-1 with Scotland away from home although, before a huge crowd of 80,000, we almost conquered them when we took the lead with a goal from Billy Hamilton. Shortly before the end, however, they equalised much to our dismay. We knew then that we had to defeat Portugal in Belfast in April 1981 to be more confident of making progress in the competition.

The game against Portugal was a tough affair and it was absolutely crucial that we came out on top. There was no score right into the second half, but things were about to change. The ball was running out of play at the corner flag. I ran and stopped it from going out, jumped over it and hit it with my left foot into the penalty area where Gerry Armstrong neatly headed it into the net. We had won this vitally important tie by that single goal, our hopes had been revived and we were now almost certain to qualify for Spain. We were all over the moon for, as you can imagine, it was quite something for such a small footballing country like Northern Ireland to proceed so far in this biggest and best of competitions. We were 'back in business' so to speak and we had been rewarded for our patience and we had given an impressive performance. There were one or two ugly scenes during the game when some hooligans in the crowd created a bit of a rumpus as well as a few blatant fouls on me which were a bit naughty, to say the least. Thankfully these incidents were soon resolved. We had played exceptionally well proving what a strong side we were becoming. We had done very well and looked forward to our progression in the competition.

But as so often happens there was a nasty sting in the tail for us. Our last game in this series of matches was against Sweden away from home in Stockholm on 3 June 1981. Before the game the manager took me aside and told me I had the skill and that I should live up to it and pull out all the stops. I knew what he was expecting of me and I was determined to do my very best. But we lost by one goal to nil and all was doom and gloom after the defeat. Added to this I had been sent off for the first time in my international career and so I automatically missed the next match. Billy Bingham had also reprimanded Jimmy Nicholl and myself for arguing with each other at the start of the match. I felt quite bad about my behaviour and was determined to set these faults behind me. It was definitely not a good day for either Northern Ireland or for Terry Cochrane and the Swedish press didn't think much of us when they declared in the morning papers that we had been a rough side and had the nerve to brand us as cowards. They even said that we had never posed any kind of a threat to them – all this from a team that was definitely not going to qualify for the 1982 World Cup finals.

It took a while to get over all this poor publicity but, after a few more scares, we did manage to qualify for the World Cup finals.

For the faithful football fans in Northern Ireland, however, we had fulfilled our greatest ambition and I myself felt sure that, despite my lapse in the Sweden match, I would be chosen to play in the World Cup finals. Once again all I could think about was all my early days of playing football in Killyleagh, Downpatrick and with the English League teams. My dream had surely now come true. I was a professional footballer; I was a First Division player; I was a Northern Ireland international and I was now on the brink of further success as a World Cup participant. It could hardly get better.

A World Cup tale from the 1978 campaign

I had been picked for the squad and we were going out to Iceland for a World Cup qualifier and were staying at a leisure centre in Largs in Ayrshire before the game. One night the lads got a bit bored and so we went into town for a few drinks. At the end of the evening we got a carry out and brought it back to my room. We had a bit of a party and the next thing was that the noise must have attracted Danny and he came in and told us to switch off the music and get to bed. Well that didn't happen, for when Danny left the room the music was back on and we were carrying on as before. Once again Danny returned and, in much stronger terms, told us to get to bed. Martin O'Neill was hiding in a cupboard when the door suddenly opened and he fell out. After that Tommy Cassidy told Danny 'we're going'. The party ended but I must say that it wasn't a binge drinking party – we were all just chilling out.

The next day, prior to leaving for Iceland, we played the Scottish under 21s. Danny picked the team and left a few of us out. We knew then that we weren't going to be playing in Reykjavik and I actually didn't even get on to the subs' bench. In the end we were beaten 1-0. When we landed back home Danny went round the lads saying he'd get in touch about the next game. Unfortunately he picked on Tommy Cassidy coming off the plane and, although Tommy had had a great season with Newcastle United, he was left out of the team. Danny told him he'd be in touch with him, but Tommy turned round and said, in no uncertain terms, 'you needn't bother'. Sadly Tommy never played for Northern Ireland again.

Sammy Nelson - my international teammate
Sammy Nelson was one of the funniest men I have ever come across. In footballing circles we called him Bruce, after Bruce Forsyth and his big chin. Sammy was playing left back one night at Windsor Park against Wales. The sun was going down over the Spion Kop end. Next thing the ball came down the line and Sammy completely missed it. He shouted over to Danny, 'Get me a pair of sunglasses. I can't see anything coming down this line'. All of us on the bench burst out laughing except Tommy Cavanagh who was, yet again, not amused.

Another time we were training at Coventry before the England game. Danny came out in these corduroy shorts that hadn't seen an iron for a very long time and to say they were creased would have been an understatement. Next thing Sammy got all the guys together and told them to keep the ball away from Danny. The game was called 'keep ball' and whoever is selected tries to get the ball off the other players. Well in forty minutes Danny never got a touch of the ball. You should have seen his face, which was bright red, and it looked as if he was about to have a heart attack. And just to rub it in, Sammy said 'You were unlucky, you nearly got a touch a couple of times'. The boys left the training ground laughing their socks off.

Team tactics usually meant Danny giving advice as to how we were going to play. But it always ended up with the senior players, including Sammy of course, having a little confab after Danny had given his tactics talk and adjusted them to the way that they were actually going to play. Danny never had a clue about the changes for the lads kept it under wraps with each player knowing what he was expected to do out on the pitch.

A game of golf

I should say first of all that I'm not a golfer. I have made a stab at playing the odd time but I never belonged to any golf club. But once, during my international days, Jimmy Nicholl, who of course played alongside me in the Northern Ireland squad, asked if I would like to come out to Balmoral Golf Club in Belfast as a chap called Fred had invited him to come and bring a friend. So I went out and enjoyed the craic with Fred, although I'm sure my golf wasn't too good. He and I got on like a house on fire and it was only later that I realised I had been playing with one of Ireland's finest ever golfers. My friend, Fred, was in fact the great Fred Daly, winner of the Open at Hoylake in 1947 and the only Northern Irishman to win the title until Rory McIlroy in 2014. But we had had a great day and Fred had obviously enjoyed my company although I don't know what he thought of my golf but, like the gentleman he was, he didn't say a word.

Fate intervenes once again

Everything was going swimmingly after these World Cup qualifiers. At the beginning of World Cup year, in March, we had a friendly international match against France at the Parc des Princes in Paris. We were beaten by four goals to nil and, after ten minutes' play, I picked up a hamstring injury. It was a great disappointment for all the players and for Billy Bingham especially when the World Cup games were coming up very soon. I wasn't getting any football at what was probably the most crucial and important part of my entire football career. Worst of all I had to come clean with the manager and declare that my injury was not responding to the excellent treatment I was receiving. Consequently, and much to my chagrin and sorrow, I could not be included in Northern Ireland's World Cup squad. It was definitely the lowest ebb in my footballing career and I found it very difficult to overcome, not only my physical injury, but more so my distress and frustration. I could only be philosophical.

Consequently I was only able to follow Northern Ireland on the television and was delighted with their magnificent performances in all their games. Our 1-0 win over the hosts, Spain, at Valencia after Gerry Armstrong's brilliant goal, as well as Pat Jennings's inspired goalkeeping after Mal Donaghy had been sent off leaving us with just ten men, is the stuff of local legend. Although we were not able to progress beyond the quarter finals I knew, as did every other person in Northern Ireland and throughout Ireland and Great Britain, that we had covered ourselves with glory and I was there when they returned to Belfast from Spain to hail them as heroes to their native soil. I knew that I had been very unlucky with my injury which had greatly disappointed Billy Bingham. He kindly arranged for me to receive the exact same money as the rest of the team had earned whilst in Spain. I thought this clearly demonstrated his affection for, and his trust, in me.

It was after this series of misfortunes that I went off on loan from Middlesbrough to play in Hong Kong. My days at Boro would soon be over.

My final opportunities to play for my country

After my game against France in March 1982 I played in just two more internationals. My twenty fifth and penultimate game for Northern Ireland was on 13 December 1983 in Belfast against Scotland. By this time I had moved from Middlesbrough to Third Division Gillingham in Kent. In the Scottish game I played the entire game and enjoyed the match which we won by two goals to nil. It was always good to beat our home rivals and this game was no exception. I had given the Scottish defence a 'roasting' and one of my brilliant runs, which Billy Hamilton turned into the Scottish goalmouth, led to Norman

Whiteside nipping in to score our first goal. And it was only another ten minutes before Sammy McIlroy added a second goal. The press verdict was that we had brushed aside Scotland and they were also full of praise for Pat Jennings, at the ripe old age of 39, who had just played his 103rd international for his country. Billy Bingham had now been in charge for 36 games, having won 14, drawn 12 and only lost 10. It felt so good to have been able, after my recent injuries and disappointments and at my now advanced age of nearly 31, to have continued to entertain the crowds as I felt I had always done. It had been, in fact, nearly two years since I had donned the green jersey and I have to say I was proud of my achievements over the years.

My swansong as an international player came in May 1984 when I made an appearance as a substitute in a 1986 World Cup qualifier in an away game against Finland. We were warned not to underestimate the Finns, not that we were ever going to for we knew they would be no pushovers. Having been what the papers described as 'the surprise packet of the 1982 finals in Spain', we set out on this campaign full of hope. But, after all this build up, we managed to lose the match by one goal to nil which was hailed as 'a Finnish nightmare' in our local papers. We were also embarrassed when we heard that Finland had only won two of their previous 23 matches. It had not been our best night of football. In what were to be my last international footballing minutes for Northern Ireland, I was reported, however, as having brought aggression to the attack and I was pleased with these end-of-career comments. I'm pleased to say that Northern Ireland once again went on to qualify for the World Cup finals in Mexico where they played against Brazil, Spain and Algeria in the group stages. They may have come fourth in their group with just a single point in their game against Algeria, but they had acquitted themselves exceedingly well on the world stage.

I was always proud of having played so many times for my country and remembered with great satisfaction that my sole international goal had come against England. I held my head high and moved on.

Receiving a gold medallion from Belfast's Lord Mayor on behalf of the IFA after Northern Ireland won the Home Championships in 1980.

See You at the Far Post

The Northern Ireland team with Dana, 1980.

With Danny Blanchflower, the Northern Ireland manager, before the Scotland match in May 1978.

In action for Northern Ireland.

With Jim Platt, showing our Northern Ireland caps.

See You at the Far Post

Northern Ireland v Denmark, 25 October 1978. We won 2-1.

Terry Cochrane

Northern Ireland squad, winners of the Home Championships, 1980.

In action for Northern Ireland.   After the Norway match, which we won 3-0.

Six

Gillingham, America and Saudi Arabia

Gillingham Football Club
When I came back from Hong Kong I knew that my days at Middlesbrough were numbered and that I was only ever likely now to be playing in their reserve team at best. It was agreed that I would go on a free transfer at the beginning of the 1983/84 season. It seems that I raised eyebrows when I agreed to join the Third Division club, Gillingham, but I was delighted that their manager, Keith Peacock, who had been a really good winger himself in his playing days, had asked me to come to Priestfield, the name of Gillingham's ground. Although he knew that I could be a bit temperamental, he judged me to be one of the most outstanding wingers in the English game. He said he needed a winger to fit into his newly shaped team and thought I could do the job. He considered me to be an entertainer and that I was the kind of player he wanted for his team. He had put up a good argument and I said I'd give it a go. My wife and boys came down to Kent and we rented a house in Parkwood up near the motorway. As a consequence 'Sir Keith', as he was affectionately known, got the best out of me and Gillingham and their fans benefitted accordingly.

Although I didn't realise it at the time, but my days at Gillingham were to be my happiest playing in the English League. I became an immediate favourite with the fans and was quickly voted their most popular player. The club had been struggling in their lowly division but the fans now had the pleasure of coming each week to see their 'joker in the pack', their 'skilful crowd pleaser' and their genuine 'big hit'. I found Keith Peacock a terrific manager to work with although many said he was on a hiding to nothing. Yet he soldiered on with a bunch of hard working players who included Martin Robinson and Dave Mehmet and the goal scoring duo of David Shearer and Tony Cascarino whom I shall mention later.

My first game was on 8 October 1983 against Preston North End and we won comfortably by two goals to nil. I scored once in this match and again in one of the next two games against Burnley and Wigan. With the skills I had brought to the club we progressed quite well but we just failed to gain promotion in each of my three years with them.

I was voted the Third Division Player of the Year in 1984, which pleased me and especially the devoted fans, and with Gillingham I made 131 appearances in the league and other matches. I scored on 21 occasions but the most memorable goal, which is still remembered to this day, came in a game against Bristol Rovers. The opposing goalkeeper knocked the ball out to me trying to clear his lines. It fell to me at the half way line and I chipped the ball 45 yards right into the net over the keeper's head. He had been completely fooled and the crowd went wild. This goal, which 'passed into legend', was voted the best goal ever seen at Gillingham. It's a pity there were no TV cameras there that day to record it but it pleases me to think that it's still remembered to this day.

There was decidedly something different about playing at Priestfield. Football was fun. I never allowed any situation to get too serious. When taking a corner when tempers were a bit frayed up there in the goalmouth, I used to slow things down by, for example, rubbing my nose on the corner flag. This immediately defused any tantrums and caused the crowd to have a laugh. During another game I felt that none of my teammates were bothering to pass the ball to me, so I left the field and sat down beside a rather bemused lady in a vacant seat in the stand and said to her that 'I might as well sit here and watch the game'. I need hardly say that the fans exploded in fits of laughter. I don't know what the team and the manager were thinking, but they never said anything. This prank of mine became a favourite with many of the Gillingham players who called it 'stand sitting' just before they took set pieces. And from time to time I would ask the referee or the linesman if he needed glasses when a decision went against me. On yet another occasion the story is told that I deliberately got myself sent off in a game in order to catch one of the supporters' buses to get me back home quicker – I'm not sure if this is a true story, probably it's not, but it does seem like something I would do.

But I have an even better story to tell you. In the middle of a game I was awarded a throw in and rushed to retrieve the ball to take a quick advantage. I grabbed the ball and it was only when it very slowly slipped out of my hand that I realised that the 'ball' was in fact a balloon. The players and fans, realising that it was a balloon, just fell about laughing. They were perhaps thinking that I might have scored quicker with the balloon than with the standard issue football. These are some real life examples which show how much fun little episodes like these can turn what is otherwise a very boring match into real entertainment.

I played in some pretty amazing games for the Gills including a third round FA tie in 1984 against Brentford at home. I had scored an equaliser early in the second half before we went 3-1 behind with less than a quarter of an hour to go. But in the last eleven minutes we scored four times and won the tie by five goals to three which was, to say the least, a most remarkable recovery. In another FA match in December 1985 against Bognor Regis, I scored one of the six goals in what was probably the biggest win for the club during my time with them. There were other not so proud moments for me, once when Dave Shearer and I were sent off in a game against Bournemouth on New Year's Day 1985, and again when I scored an own goal in March 1986. But these incidents were easily overshadowed by the great performances I regularly put in for the club.

The centenary game
In 1994, years after I had left the club, I was invited, with lots of other former players, to Gillingham's centenary celebrations. There was of course a wonderful banquet with 420 guests, but the highlight was a match between two teams of former players. I played for Keith Peacock's team and, at the tender age of just 41, I was one of the younger players on the field. The opposition team was under another former manager, Ernie Morgan. The game produced twelve goals with Ernie's team winning by seven goals to five. The oldest man on the field was 75-year-old Charlie Marks who scored a penalty for his team. It seems he scored another penalty in 1955 against Northampton which broke the net. The net remained intact this time however. In the newspaper reports I'm glad to say that I was mentioned a few times. My shirt was characteristically flapping around my shorts; I was regularly running half the length of the field doing my usual stepovers and shimmies. And I scored one of my team's goals. It had been a day to remember and I was delighted to have been part of it.

People and fun at Gillingham

When we first arrived we quickly got to know our neighbours, Malcolm and Denise Hobbs. They were great people who soon made us feel at home. As I have said before you've got to be happy not only with the club but also with the folk you live with. We used to hold parties and some of them were a bit wild. Once the owner of the local pub in Rainham came up for a barbecue with some of his customers who were Gills fans. My brother-in-law Tommy and my sister, June, were staying with us for the weekend and he agreed to organise the barbecue while the rest of us had a drink. Little did we realise that Tommy was drinking too and the more he drank the more the food on the barbecue was getting burnt. By the end of the evening, everyone was so sozzled that it turned out to be the only barbecue that any of us had ever attended where nobody got any food.

David Shearer came down to the club from the Boro and, as I was a former teammate of his, I was assigned to look after him and he stayed with me for a while. One morning I got a call from the Derbyshire police asking if I had a David Shearer staying with me and I confirmed that I had. The sergeant replied, saying 'Not any more – we have him'. He then asked me if I had a car, and again I confirmed that I had. The sergeant then asked me to check if it was in the garage or parked outside the house. I went to check and it wasn't there. It was obvious that Shakey had taken the car to go to Boro for the weekend. The sergeant then went on to say that he'd crashed the car at a place called Ripley. He said he'd phone me back in 15 minutes and, in the meantime, I contacted the club chairman, Charlie Cox, who then was quickly in touch with the club's solicitor. The advice I then got after these conversations was that I should tell the police that Shakey had stolen the car. When the police phoned back I told him and left it to them. When Shakey came back he apologised and the car was repaired. Keith Peacock asked me if I wanted him to sack Shakey but I said 'No'. I knew why he had taken the car and that he now had paid the price for his stupidity. I didn't see any reason to punish him anymore and besides he was doing a great job in the team regularly scoring goals. David eventually joined me playing in the Northern League at Billingham at the end of his career before returning to his home in Scotland.

Steve Bruce and I were great friends when I joined the Gills and he was already on their books. He and his wife made us welcome and we went out on a couple of nights and enjoyed their company. I remember one night when we were going out leaving their dog in our house until we got back. Well when we did return there was blood all over the house and it looked just like a slaughterhouse. It seems that the dog had cut its tail and had shaken it all over certain parts of the house. I can tell you it took some cleaning remembering, as I said previously, that we had rented the house. Later in his career, Steve went on to play for Manchester United and ended up managing four clubs, Huddersfield Town, Wigan Athletic and Crystal Palace. At the time of writing he is manager of Hull City FC.

Bill 'Buster' Collins was Mr Gillingham. He was a very sociable man who was from Northern Ireland and he and I clicked right away. He was the club's physiotherapist and every time you had a niggle or a more serious injury, you went to see him not only to get treatment but also to get a tale or two out of him. I got to know him and his wife well and I still have warm memories of both of them. I think clubs need people like Buster who was the life and soul of what Gillingham FC stood for.

Tony Cascarino and Dave Mehmet were two lads who were always together. Dave was skipper of the team and acted like Tony's mentor. He bought a pub in Gillingham where we used to hang out and he was always wheeling and dealing in lots of so-called deals. They were good lads and in the changing room the banter with them was good. Dave would say something and Tony would agree and hang on Dave's every word. The years have now gone by and I see Tony on Sky TV and I think that Dave must be behind him somewhere in the background telling him what to say. You've heard the saying 'the lights are on but there is nobody at home' – well I shall say no more.

The team was unlucky in the three seasons I was with them for we finished in the top four and if play-offs had been around at the time, we would have been in them. The likes of Steve Bruce, Martin Robinson, Tony Cascarino and Dave Mehmet, whom I have already mentioned, were all in the team and in one of those seasons we took Everton to three games in the FA Cup. The Medway towns are commuter towns with people travelling to and from London to work and to support the London clubs. Gillingham at best drew a crowd of around 6,000 but when we played Everton there were 16,000 spectators, thus showing that lots of the locals came out of their closets to watch us play in an FA Cup match.

I'd like to thank the staff at the Gills. I met so many wonderful people both at the football club and in the social club where we used to have a great time with the fans with whom we always socialised. I can't remember all their names but they will know who they are and how much we enjoyed being with them.

I left Gillingham at the end of the 1985/86 season having thoroughly enjoyed my time with such a fine bunch of teammates and their enthusiastic fans. In these seasons, as I have already said, the team had got quite close to promotion so I felt I had contributed well to their overall improvement in the English League with my many good performances. By way of a fitting farewell I was acknowledged by both press and fans alike 'the most exciting player most of them had ever seen at the club' and the player whose sheer entertainment value was incalculable. And I have only recently heard that I have been voted into the Gills Greatest XI and this is the ringing endorsement which went with the accolade.

'Attacking midfielder – Terry Cochrane – a wing wizard and consummate entertainer, blessed with bags of skill, the Northern Ireland international winger was signed from Middlesbrough on a free transfer by Keith Peacock in 1983, and crowned his debut with a goal in a 2-0 win over Preston at Priestfield. His three seasons at the club saw the Gills challenging for promotion every year, with one of the most attractive, attacking squads ever assembled at the club and he was a worthy winner of our Player of the Year trophy in 1984/85'.

With this acclamation ringing in my ears I went off to make my final two appearances for Northern Ireland. But my football career had still further to go.

Dallas Sidekicks

In 1986 another opportunity knocked. This time I was invited to go to play in the American professional soccer league with the Dallas Sidekicks in Texas. The team had just been founded in 1984 so was a new venture for their city. This time I was able to bring my family with me and I was pleased about that. My sons, Paul and Steven, were now 11 and 8 respectively and were excited about going stateside. Etta was delighted as well.

Playing soccer in America was something that quite a lot of slightly older former professionals, including the mercurial George Best, joined in the twilight of their careers. I was now 33 years old but still felt very fit and looked forward to this new opportunity. My offer to join the Sidekicks came from Gordon Jago who, as a Charlton player in the 1950s and the manager for Millwall and Queen's Park Rangers, was very well respected on the world soccer scene and I got to know and value his enthusiasm and experience whilst I was over there.

But although the people were friendly, the football was different, to say the least. I had never before played league football indoors. The Sidekicks' home venue was a large stadium which doubled as a basketball arena. And the football was not exactly 'regulation'. Although there were eleven players on each team, they played in rotation with only seven or so of them on the 'field' at any one time. I actually found this format quite off putting although I played to the very best of my ability. I didn't think this was the game for me although the lads on my team were totally committed. The crowds, often as many as 9,000 of them, packed tightly into this steaming cauldron, went absolutely crazy about their team and followed them through thick and thin. During the 1986 season when I was with them, the Sidekicks' slogan was 'The Wild Side of Soccer'.

I only stayed in Dallas for five months. I did take the opportunity along with my family to visit a few of the neighbouring cities and places of interest. When playing away games with the Sidekicks, we went to such cities as Wichita and Memphis. Unfortunately I didn't make enough time to visit Elvis Presley's Graceland home when I was in Memphis which was a shame.

I returned to England after this American footballing interlude, which I could only put down to one of life's interesting experiences.

Millwall and Hartlepool - a fond farewell to professional football
I was hardly back from America when I got a call to sign for Millwall. I jumped at the opportunity and was pleased to play for them the very first week after my arrival. I was pleased to see that Teddy Sheringham, the England international, was also on the team. We went to play Birmingham City and we won the game by one goal to nil and it was my cross which set up the score. At the beginning of the following week I went out with my teammates to train but unfortunately got a pretty nasty Achilles tendon injury which, I'm

afraid, put paid to my days at Millwall. And so, after only a couple of games, I was out of the game once again.

I then got the chance to go and play for Hartlepool but after just two games for them, I suffered a hamstring injury and I had to leave. My days of playing professional soccer in the English League were over.

I now saw a move to amateur football as the natural progression for me. I had enjoyed many years with so many clubs in so many different parts of the world. There had been those large and boisterous crowds cheering me on both at club and international level. I had then had the wonderful chance to savour the more exotic game, so to speak, in America, Hong Kong and later on, in Saudi Arabia. It was time, therefore, to hang up my professional boots and see what the amateur game had to offer.

To be honest I was looking forward to this slightly more leisurely paced game. I was now in my mid 30s and, after those rather very short periods at Millwall and Hartlepool, I now set my eyes on a different goal.

Coaching in Saudi Arabia

Early in 1991, by which time I was all of 38 years old and playing in the northern amateur league, I happened to notice an advertisement in the *Daily Mirror* which greatly interested me. Football coaches were being sought for the Saudi Arabian military. This sounded absolutely intriguing and I quickly got in touch with the prospective employers, Saudi American Sports. They were interviewing in London and when I arrived I was almost immediately offered the position although I had to have an Aids test which didn't exactly fill me with the joys of spring especially when the doctor said he 'would be in touch'. However I was pleased to have been appointed to the job but wondered what I was letting myself in for, knowing that there would be plenty of pros and cons in accepting the job. Firstly I would not be allowed to bring my family with me and secondly the appointment was for the most of one year. I talked this over with Etta and the boys and they encouraged me to go – they would miss me but they knew what a great opportunity this was. So I accepted and soon found myself in the sands of Arabia – well actually in the capital, Riyadh, where I was processed by the company and had another Aids test. I had been in most parts of the world but this was definitely another very different setting for a boy from Killyleagh.

After about a month I was posted to the ancient city of Jedda where my job was to coach the players on the base to form a team to represent the Saudi military against other regiments elsewhere. The soldiers were good enough footballers and I'm glad to say that I was able to greatly improve their skills. They knew they had an international player of some worth as their coach and they were as determined to learn from me as I was to teach them.

However soon after my arrival I realised there was a problem. There was the Gulf War raging and my trainee footballers were often suddenly being called away to fight on the front line on the borders of Kuwait. This meant that one day I had a full squad of players and the next none at all. Consequently I ended up doing coaching sessions for the other people who were on the base including the officers, the soldiers not being sent out to fight, the cadets and some local youths. I had to train each group separately as there was no integration. Working with the cadets was an unusual experience for they would turn up on the pitch wearing hobnailed boots and then proceed to kick seven bells out of each other. I was told later that these lads had been recruited from the desert and, apart from learning about army procedures, they had still to learn how to use a knife and fork. And, just as importantly for me, I had to teach them how to kick the ball and not the man.

I therefore had time on my hands but this did not prove to be any real hardship in such a country as Saudi Arabia. At the fabulous stadium where the training took place, which incidentally could hold over 30,000 spectators, there was an Olympic sized swimming pool and many fitness suites. I was allowed to use these facilities and I made full use of them as I waited for my young charges to return.

But there was another side to spending my off duty time. Weekends in the Middle East were Thursdays and Fridays rather than Saturdays and Sundays and this took a bit of getting used to. I got to know Jim Brandon really well. He was the basketball coach and was about 6' 19" tall and had captained the Boston Celtics and Sunderland. We used to go to some of the parties in the compounds where some of the other lads lived but, as there were no bars, the guys made home brew and drank the local drink called sadiki. This was absolutely lethal and many of the lads got quite drunk on it.

Some Thursday nights after work, the Filipinos who worked with us on the base would take us fishing. We would travel by minibus for a couple of hours into the desert and park by the Red Sea. The guys had all the gear and all we needed to take with us were our sleeping bags. We then prepared a fire and waited for the lads to supply the fish and other seafood to eat. Lying on the beach under the stars beside the Red Sea was a genuinely surreal experience considering that there was a war going on and I just took time to reflect and think about the difference between being back home and being here in war torn Saudi Arabia.

I made many other friends too, many of whom were American nationals, and one who was the King's chief helicopter pilot who had, from time to time and at the drop of a hat, to leave to attend to his Sovereign's wishes. In such a wealthy country there were countless receptions for the foreigners who were living in the compound and I was often invited. This was certainly quite different from any receptions I had been invited to at home or in England. Often members of the Saudi Royal family were present and I had the pleasure and honour of meeting some of them. I even saw King Fahd at one of these functions. I would never forget these extraordinary experiences for I knew how privileged I had been.

Unfortunately I was not able to visit any other parts of the Kingdom – I suppose mainly on account of the war – but I was able to explore every part of the fabulous and exciting city of Jedda. To have spent this year not only improving the footballing skills of the lads in the military but also to have encountered this rarefied atmosphere in the Middle East, was yet another 'never to be forgotten' episode in my life to date. Meeting a royal personage was quite a step up from the lovely ordinary Irish and English people whom I had met thus far. Above all, the young soldiers had become very competent soccer players and I had the great satisfaction of knowing that many of them would go on to play international matches themselves for their country and many of them did, in fact, do so.

Spending this year in Saudi Arabia in the heat of the desert without my family with me had been a lonely experience and I was glad to return home. I knew, however, that I had made a success of my time there and, in later days, a number of the young Saudis would thank me for what I had taught them. Perhaps, like me, they had put into practice the thrill of going forward with the ball and appreciating my maxim – 'when you get the ball, go forward'. I'm sure they did for I know that, since I was there in the early 1990s, football has taken off in Saudi Arabia. The national team has played in four World Cup competitions right up to 2006 and have successfully participated in various Asian Cup games. There are currently 30 teams in the Saudi First Division and many Saudis are playing for teams in Europe. Perhaps I sowed the little footballing acorn that has developed into a mighty Saudi soccer oak.

Terry Cochrane

With my son Steven, then aged 6, acting as mascot when I was playing for Gillingham against Derby in 1985.

Scoring against Burnley, 1983-84 season.

Gillingham v Blackpool, 1985-86 season.

Terry Cochrane

Gillingham v Bournemouth, 1986-87 season.

In action for Gillingham.

See You at the Far Post

Player profile photo from Roger Triggs' Gillingham book.

Gillingham trophies 1984-85 season: Player of the Year, Players' Player of the Year, Fans Player of the Year, Media Player of the Year.

Terry Cochrane

In Saudi Arabia, 1991.

Seven

Professional to Amateur

Playing in the Amateur League
I had now retired from the professional league and decided to enjoy the game in the amateur league. I joined a team with a very classy name – Billingham Synthonia, or the 'Synners' as they were nicknamed. They were a good outfit and their manager was Tony Lee who had a great reputation in the Northern League. For five years I played every week in front of their small, but enthusiastic, crowds who really enjoyed watching the teams in the Northern Amateur League. With me as an essential and regular member of the team, we made a lot of progress during those years. The lads there were great fun and keen about their football. We won the 2nd division title and in the next year, we were crowned champions of the 1st division. And in 1989 Billingham won their equivalent of the English title and this was the only English cup I was to win in my entire career. I was enjoying my football now into my middle to late 30s although I have to admit that it was becoming a bit more of a struggle to keep playing, at least to the standards I had been used to.

I then joined, in the early 1990s, a club called Marske United, based in a village close to Redcar on the coast and not very far away from Middlesbrough. In those days the Seasiders, as they were known, were playing in the Wearside League and doing well. In the 1994/95 season, they were league champions and League Cup winners, before then being promoted to the Northern League. The club secretary, John Corner, was delighted to have signed me on. He seemed to know a bit about me and that I was not, in his words, a know-it-all. He looked forward to me showing what he called my 'magic' on the pitch and sharing my experience with the younger lads. He also declared that he was glad there was no mention of money and was a bit surprised to hear that I only drank orange juice after the game. It was a win-win situation and I had great fun turning out every Saturday to play with guys who wanted to learn and fans who appreciated the type of game I played. Heading off to Marske on a Saturday was certainly much better than sitting at home twiddling my thumbs.

For a few months in 1992, I joined another team in the Northern League where I got my first taste of managerial experience as player manager. South Bank United, known as the Bankers, was reputed to be the oldest football club in the north east of England founded in 1868. Sadly the club, after two arson attacks on their ground and social club in 1991, could no longer remain in the league and had to close down. The lads there had tried hard to do some renovations to the ground and the changing rooms and to bring back the football people in the area but unfortunately they were not too well thought of and security was a big problem. They got a very fierce Alsatian guard dog which I wouldn't go near. It was chained up but the intruders just pinched the chain and the dog as well. The groundsman had a tractor to keep the pitch cut and even it was stolen. My stay at South Bank was short but it certainly had its moments.

I then went to Ferryhill Athletic but didn't stay there long either. This club, too, had financial and other troubles which led to its departure from the league in the late 1990s. I felt I had learnt a great deal from my short time with these two clubs and wondered if I might ever get the chance to manage a more senior side. I felt ready for it, but wondered whether any club would take me on.

I then had an interesting offer from a friend of mine, Steve Gibson, who still is, associated with Middlesbrough. Steve owned a company called Bulkhaul and the firm had its own football team which regularly played in the Sunday amateur league in the north east of England. Steve invited me to play for Bulkhaul and I enjoyed both the games and the camaraderie with the lads on the team. I continued to play for them for at least fifteen years. There was a great team spirit and they had a few ex pros like Archie Stephens and Gary Gill, ex Boro, and myself, and such was the quality of the team, that we were hardly ever beaten.

We were doing so well that Steve thought he would broaden our horizons by taking us to Germany to play the regiments and there were, of course, plenty of funny stories about things that happened during these visits. I remember seeing a water barrel at the corner of the pitch and so we asked the army lads what it was used for. They then told us that Mark Page, who was the DJ on the Forces Radio and who set up a lot of their games, was always winding them up. So they got their own back by ducking him in this barrel. The soldiers were delighted that they had at last got one over on him but I can tell you that Mark was definitely not amused.

The team also regularly headed off each year to Cyprus and Mark again came with us. We were playing at a place called Protaras and afterwards the army lads brought us back to their club that was right beside the sea. It was a really nice place but the strange thing about it was that all the seats were coloured white except for a single one that was blue. Unfortunately Mark didn't notice that he was sitting on the blue seat. The next thing was that one of the army lads got up and welcomed us to the club and said that there was a tradition that anyone sitting on the blue chair must pay a forfeit. Mark, by now realising that he was on the blue seat, tried to get up but unfortunately two big army lads held him down. They then picked him up on the chair and took him down to the water's edge and threw him in. He was, yet again, not at all amused.

There was another time when Archie, Gary and I were on the beach having a bit of a sleep and generally lazing around. Gilly (Gary) had bought a book and had his nose in it all the time. Archie and I were getting a bit miffed as he wasn't joining in our conversations and this was the pattern over the next few days. But once he did get up and go to the bar to buy us some drinks so, while he was a way, I picked up his book and tore out the last two pages and put them in my pocket. Nothing was said for days by which time we were sure he must have reached the end of his book. Archie and I kept a close eye on him to see if it had dawned on him that the last two pages were gone. Naturally we wanted to know how the story ended and, as we were about to return home, we asked him if the book had been any good and how had it ended. He just looked at us and said it had been a great book although it had a very strange ending. Archie and I kept our faces straight and, after we had arrived back home, we got those last two pages laminated and sent to him. I'll not say what he called us knowing that he had told us about the book's strange ending – and now knowing the reason why.

This was definitely what suited me at this stage of my life – a more leisurely brand of soccer with a little light training and unhurried football – and all topped off with time to relax on the beach or in the pool and have fun with my friends. Steve once took me to Singapore to play in a tournament there and we stayed for a week in the world famous Raffles Hotel. I was forever grateful to Steve for giving me the chance to visit so many terrific places.

I suppose it could be said that I had arrived at an elegant conclusion to my football playing career and, apart from the occasional charity match, I saw my future, not in playing any more football myself, but having the opportunity to put back into the game what I had learned over the years from my early days in Killyleagh and Downpatrick. With this goal in mind, I prepared to study for my coaching certificate.

Eight

Coaching

For years now I have held the coveted UEFA 'A' licence which qualifies me as a coach. After hanging up my boots, I got a job as football development officer with Spennymoor Council which entailed me getting the local community involved in the sport. For five years I visited up to twenty schools in the area and, from the youngsters who were participating in the scheme, I selected players, both boys and girls, to represent the district in competitive matches during the school holidays. Over the years I was able to arrange games with teams from the likes of Newcastle, Sunderland, Middlesbrough and Hartlepool. The Council supplied a bus so that the parents of the players could come to the away games and watch the matches. I was also able to arrange a tour of the various clubs for them to see how they were run and to get a glimpse of how professional footballers prepared for their matches down in their changing rooms.

However when the Council went over budget and needed to make economies, they pulled the plug and I was out of a job. But all was not lost, for since my time coaching at Spennymoor, lots of the local youth clubs have taken up my ideas, taken further steps forward and continued to arrange matches involving the kids of the area. And one of the best things about the scheme I had started was the introduction to the game of Luke Williams and David Atkinson, both of whom I am pleased to say have furthered their careers with Middlesbrough Football Club.

Much later, in 2008, after leaving the manager's job at Glenavon, Colin Telfer, who was manager of Rosario FC in Belfast, asked me to join them as first team coach. I thought it would be a good opportunity and I took the job. This meant that I was still able to stay at home with my mother in Killyleagh. The club was based on the Ormeau Road and had lots of students in the team. Colin was doing a good job and we had a great first season winning promotion to the next division, something they had never done in their history. So it was a good time both for the club and for Colin and myself. However the job didn't last very long, after I got a call to manage the Hartlepool Ladies at East Durham College. This greatly appealed to me so I was off home again to try my luck with a ladies' team. Unfortunately it was a brief stay although the ladies trained well and played good football in the few matches they had whilst I was there. But fate intervened once more when Hartlepool FC withdrew their funding and I was jobless yet again.

In retrospect I think I have walked under too many ladders in my coaching career – but it was worth it.

Broadcasting

I have commentated on local Teesside radio over many years on matches involving teams like Hartlepool and Darlington. I really like being able to describe the game that I know and love so well to many housebound fans who can no longer get out to see their teams. I think my style of being informative and full of fun is something they enjoy and they tell me that the game really comes alive when I am at the microphone.

The boat story

In 2007 I was asked by the owner of one of the entertainment ships on the Tees to see if I could help him move the ship over to Belfast. We went over there with high hopes but, after various meetings with the harbourmaster, he wouldn't budge from his stance that he would not grant a permanent mooring for the ship in the harbour. We persisted and approached some people in authority in the city, including the then Lord Mayor, Jim Rodgers, whom I had known from my footballing days. We were invited to his parlour at the City Hall where we each received a gift from him. Then we spoke to Peter Robinson MP, because the ship would have been moored close to the city centre within his East Belfast constituency. It had been pretty difficult to get an interview with Robinson who said he would only help us if we were granted a mooring for the ship. But as we didn't get the mooring, the whole venture foundered. But nevertheless the trips we had made to Belfast in our endeavours were memorable and we were grateful for all the hospitality we received.

Encounters with other footballing heroes

People constantly ask me about the big names in football whom I met during my career. I have already mentioned lots of them including those lads who played for Northern Ireland and also the likes of Bobby Moore and Trevor Brooking. But everyone asks that question 'Did you ever meet George Best?' Well I certainly did and there was a time in the early 1980s that I knew him quite well. In those days when I was playing for Northern Ireland in the games coming up to the 1982 World Cup I knew that, although George was at the end of his professional career, he had been approached by Billy Bingham to play in the team as well. It didn't quite come off but he was around and would have seen me play. I was on the bench on 12 October 1977 when George played his 37th and last game for his country against the Netherlands in Belfast. I remember some brief encounters with the player who was considered Northern Ireland's greatest footballing legend. And I also recall him buying me a drink at the Chimney Corner Hotel outside Belfast. But I suppose my greatest memory was actually playing with George in a testimonial match for Jim Platt against Sunderland at Ayresome Park in September 1981. I remember the game and thought that I had played pretty well but the greatest delight was being in a team with the great George Best for the entire ninety minutes.

Coaching younsters at the Kick Summer Camp 1988/89.

Terry Cochrane

With Steve Gibson and the former minister of Sport, Kate Hoey, at Bulkhaul in 2000.

South Bank player/manager 1996.

Nine

Management at last

Glenavon Football Club

I had always wanted to try my luck and get a manager's post but nothing ever seemed to come my way – at least not in the professional game. Then I saw that the Glenavon post was up for grabs and I applied for the job early in January 2008 after their previous manager, Colin Malone, had been sacked. It seems there were 19 applicants for the post and I was pleased that I came out on top. I'm sure I landed the job because of my previous professional background as well as having the requisite coaching qualifications. I was determined not to let this opportunity slip and I immediately set about bringing in new ideas and a new training regime which was much needed, and appreciated by, the players. I told the press that I intended to take the club by the scruff of the neck and move forward. I looked forward to exciting times at Mourneview Park, our ground in Lurgan, county Armagh and to staying with, and looking after, my mother back in Killyleagh.

When I arrived at the club, the board members explained to me that their goal was to ensure Glenavon's survival in the league in order for them to rebuild for the coming season. Since four of the clubs in the league were soon to be excluded to shorten it, it was my job to make sure the club survived the cut.

The team clearly needed to improve and I was determined to bring in some new players although this idea didn't prove to be too popular. Some of the early results were disappointing. The first time I watched the lads play at home shortly after my arrival, they were beaten 2-1 by Bangor. This was followed by an even worse result – a 6-3 defeat by Loughgall in the Mid Ulster Cup. I did my best to encourage the lads and we did have a few wins thereafter, including a satisfying 2-0 win over Institute. By the middle of March we were, if not exactly on a winning streak, definitely getting better results. I kept optimistic and told the team how much they were improving. Probably the best win to date was against local rivals, Portadown, whom we had not defeated for seven years and everyone, particularly our loyal fans, were delighted. The last game of the season produced the biggest win since I had arrived – a 5-0 drubbing of Armagh City. The lads were, by now, oozing confidence and I was really looking forward to the new season. I had also introduced a new youth policy, which was proving to be a great success.

But, in June, after just five months in the job and despite the fact that I was clearly making some progress, I got the sack. You do well and get sacked – that's the Irish for you! The papers said that I had left by mutual consent but I do know that my successors also only lasted six months as well before they, too, were shown the door. I felt vindicated for I knew I had done a good job in my short time with the club and I had enjoyed the experience and was sad to leave. I wished Glenavon well for the future as I left Northern Ireland and returned to England.

Ten

Signing off

Looking back on my career has been a great experience, both for life in general and for football in particular. Over these years I have met many wonderful people and visited lots of interesting countries which has helped me achieve my early ambitions in the world of football. The fans at the three clubs where I spent the bulk of my career, Burnley, Middlesbrough and Gillingham, have been great. You hear of players who have been given a hard time by the fans but I must say that I have been most fortunate to be liked by the fans of all these three clubs.

The ultimate accolade in football is to be capped by your country and to score against the old enemy, England, at Wembley. These are the memories that you can never forget - as I was told by my Northern Ireland teammate, Sammy McIlroy, who played for Manchester United. The question that people still ask me is what I would be worth in today's football climate. I always answer by saying that it wouldn't really matter if you could just continue to play and enjoy the game. To me the most important thing is playing football and not, as often happens nowadays, firstly asking how much you were going to be paid as soon as you join a club, rather than training for, and getting ready for, your first game. I do find it frustrating when I hear them ask for their money before they have even kicked a ball. I hope, like me, that everyone will remember the people at each of the clubs I represented with fondness and lots of good memories. There have been many people whom I have come to like and respect and who have become friends for life and not just as part of my footballing career. The fans can watch you play on a Saturday and judge your football skills, but it's the life after the match that turns these ardent fans into lifelong friends and that's what really counts as far as I am concerned.

I think these quotes will sum up just how much I enjoyed the game and how much I set out to entertain the faithful fans who watched me week in, week out.

> *Cochrane was an old fashioned winger who liked nothing better than taking on full backs. The Northern Ireland international teased and tormented opponents with skilful runs and a deceptive body swerve coupled with speed and guile. More of a goal maker than taker, he could also score spectacular goals.*

> *The County Down wing wizard made defenders' lives a living hell as he bobbed, weaved and scampered down the flanks.*

> *The sight of Terry Cochrane, with his socks round his ankles showing his shin free legs, will be something no less respecting fan will ever forget.*

David Healy and me, with my nephews Christopher and Andrew, at the unveiling of the Killyleagh footballers' mural, 2006.